PATTON

MILITARY PROFILES

SERIES EDITOR

Dennis E. Showalter, Ph.D.
Colorado College

Instructive summaries for general and expert
readers alike, volumes in the Military Profiles
series are essential treatments of significant and
popular military figures drawn from world history,
ancient times through the present.

PATTON

Legendary Commander

Martin Blumenson
and Kevin Hymel

Potomac Books, Inc.
Washington, D.C.

Library of Congress Cataloging-in-Publication Data
Blumenson, Martin.
  Patton : legendary commander / Martin Blumenson and Kevin Hymel.
— 1st ed.
      p. cm. — (Military profiles)
  Includes bibliographical references and index.
  ISBN 978-1-57488-762-4 (hardcover : alk. paper) — ISBN 978-1-
57488-763-1 (pbk. : alk. paper)
  1. Patton, George S. (George Smith), 1885–1945. 2. Generals—United
States—Biography. 3. United States. Army—Biography. 4. United
States—History, Military—20th century. 5. World War, 1939–1945—
Campaigns. I. Hymel, Kevin, 1966– II. Title.
  E745.P3B545 2008
  355'.0092—dc22
  [B]
                            2008009336

Printed in the United States of America on acid-free paper that meets
the American National Standards Institute Z39-48 Standard.

Potomac Books, Inc.
22841 Quicksilver Drive
Dulles, Virginia 20166

First Edition

10 9 8 7 6 5 4 3 2 1

Contents

Preface

Shortly after World War II, when the Allies interrogated Field Marshal Gerd von Rundstedt, the senior commander who opposed the Allied invasion of France, they asked him to rate the skills of his opponents. He is reputed to have said, "Patton. He was your best."

Praise for his performance was precisely what George Smith Patton Jr. had wished for and sought all his life. As a child, he aspired to be a soldier, a fighting man. As a youngster, he imagined himself to be a lieutenant general. In school, his written exercises revealed his identification with the military and his knowledge of tactics, intelligence, and maneuver. At age eighteen, he was already searching for what he called the "undefinable difference" that distinguished "a great general from a merely good one."[1]

As a cadet at the Virginia Military Institute and the U.S. Military Academy, Patton applied himself intensely to learning the fundamentals of his profession. He acquired more knowledge and competence in his early assignments in Illinois and Washington, D.C. Striving to become widely known in the Army, he entered horse shows, raced, and played polo. He competed in the 1912 Olympic Games and was a well-known swordsman.[2]

The highlight of his early service was his work along the Mexican border as a member of Gen. John J. Pershing's Punitive Expedition into Mexico. What must have seemed to him to be the culminating experience was his participation in World War I, first with Pershing's headquarters and later as the foremost American tank expert in Europe as well as in the entire U.S. Army.

The twenty years of peace between the wars were for Patton a time of anxious waiting. He sharpened his military skills and expanded his understanding of warfare, but he suffered from the absence of conflict and feared he was growing too old to fulfill what he called his fate or destiny. His reassignment to the tanks in 1940 marked the beginning of his rise to worldwide fame. Promoted quickly from commanding a brigade to a division, then an armored corps, he drew attention to himself by his participation in the large-scale maneuvers in Tennessee, the Carolinas, Louisiana, and Texas. He created and managed a vast Desert Training Center in the southwestern United States.

Finally, he was selected to lead the U.S. troops designated to invade French Morocco in November 1942, as part of the Allied Operation Torch, the Anglo-American descent on French Northwest Africa. Patton's success in that venture and his subsequent transfer to command the U.S. II Corps in Tunisia, after the American defeat in the Battle of Kasserine Pass, added to his reputation.[3]

He next commanded the U.S. Seventh Army in the invasion and campaign of Sicily. His efforts were a triumph of mobility and audacity. Unfortunately, toward the end of the fighting, he slapped two hospitalized soldiers, assuming they were malingering. He thereby lost the possibility of commanding the American forces in the Normandy invasion.

Relegated to idleness in Sicily for more than four months, Patton finally received the call to report to England. There he took command of the Third Army and prepared his units for their follow-up role in Operation Overlord. He was almost sent home in disgrace when his presence, which was supposed to be secret, was revealed in a speech he gave in Knutsford, England. The misunderstanding blew over, and Patton entered battle in Normandy on August 1, 1944, almost two months after D-Day. Patton's Third Army, activated at a time of great operational fluidity on the continent, sparked the war of movement and turned a local breakthrough into a theater-wide breakout.

He was the focal point in the maneuver to close the Argentan-Falaise pocket and the first to reach and cross the Seine River. He led the exhilarating pursuit of the German forces across northern France until gasoline shortages forced him to stop at the Meuse River.

The autumn fighting was difficult around Metz and Nancy. But the German surprise attack, the Battle of the Bulge on December 16, 1944, brought Patton his sublime moment. He turned part of his army of about 300,000 men forty-five degrees from an eastward orientation to northward, attacking the flank of the salient created by the German advance. His men reached and relieved the encircled American soldiers at Bastogne and had much to do with turning the Germans back and erasing their gains.[4]

Patton's army crossed the Rhine River, overran much of Bavaria and Austria, and finished the war in Czechoslovakia. Gen. Dwight D. Eisenhower, the Supreme Allied Commander, wrote to him early in 1945, "You have made your Army a fighting force that is not excelled . . . by any other of equal size in the world." Patton was termed in 1948 "the outstanding exponent of . . . combat effectiveness in World War II."[5]

Assigned to occupy Bavaria after the war, Patton found himself unsympathetic with American policy. He opposed nonfraternization with the Germans and the punishment of Nazi Party members. Because of his obstinacy, Eisenhower relieved him of command of the Third Army and transferred him to the Fifteenth Army, which was writing the lessons learned from the war.

About to depart the theater for Christmas leave at home, Patton was involved in a freak automobile accident. Paralyzed, he lingered in the hospital for eleven days before dying on December 21, 1945. The official announcement of his death the following day carried this tribute: "Probably no soldier has had a greater compliment paid him than that given General Patton by his most powerful and skillful opponents. He was termed the ablest American field commander faced by the German Army on any front."[6]

An American folk hero, Patton has been both loved and disparaged—loved by those who worked for him and understood his exuberance, warmth, and devotion and disparaged by those who knew him less and "loathed him for his harsh methods, his overbearing personality, his arrogance, his profanity and the sheer wrath of his temper."[7] Half cowboy, uncouth and provincial, and half sophisticate, cultured and at ease in the highest social strata, the man behind the legend was a complex and paradoxical person, full of self-doubt and moodiness, who tried to remake himself into his image of a warrior. He was uniquely American, indubitably so, "and it is hard to imagine any other nation producing a general exactly"—even remotely—"like him."[8] He was the best American combat general this nation produced.

Martin Blumenson did not live to see the completion of this book, but we did work together on it every Wednesday night until he could work no more. He had no peer when it came to understanding Patton, and it was an education seeing him work.

Other people contributed to this book. At the top of that list is Merry Pantano, who brought Martin and me together for this project. Martin was originally set to write the book but declined. I told Merry that I would help him just to have the opportunity to work with him. She set up the whole project, and Martin made sure we were coauthors.

I owe a special thanks to my mother and father, my biggest fans. My mother, Alice Hymel, proved to be an excellent editor and looked at the book from a nonmilitary historian's point of view. My pop, Gary Hymel, an author in his own right, continually encouraged me to complete the book and edited it twice. Roger Cirillo gave the manuscript a critical review. My friends Orrie Rondinella, Paul Karpers, Geoff Emigh, John McManus, Benjamin Harvey, Cole Kingseed, Cyd Upson, and Chris Anderson also offered advice and encouragement. Ann Volk and George Sutherland provided me a place to stay while I completed the manuscript.

The folks at Potomac Books were helpful as always. Claire Noble encouraged me to finish this book. She is incredibly professional, and I consider her a friend. Rick Russell helped get the book off the ground. Jen Waldrop kept everything running smoothly. Julie Kimmel and Katie Freeman made sense of the text. Sam Dorrance answered all my inquiries.

All opinions and interpretations expressed in this book are the authors' alone and all errors, both of omission and commission, the authors' responsibility.

Chronology

1885   George Smith Patton Jr. is born November 11, San Gabriel, Los Angeles County, to George Smith and Ruth Wilson Patton.

1897   Attends Stephen Cutter Clark's Classical School for Boys in Pasadena, California.

1903   Enters the Virginia Military Institute, Lexington, Virginia, as a cadet.

1904   Enters the U.S. Military Academy, West Point, New York, as a cadet.

1909   Commissioned second lieutenant, Cavalry, and joins the Fifteenth Cavalry at Fort Sheridan, Illinois.

1910   Marries Beatrice Banning Ayer on May 26.

1911   Daughter Beatrice Ayer Patton is born on March 19. Patton is transferred to Fort Myer, Virginia.

1912   Participates in the Modern Pentathlon in the Olympic Games in Stockholm, Sweden, June 7–July 17. Receives instruction in fencing in Samur, France (July–September), and completes the first-year fencing course at the Mounted Service School, Fort Riley, Kansas, September 23.

1914   Completes the second-year fencing course at the Mounted Service School.

1915   Daughter Ruth Ellen Patton is born on March 1. Patton joins the Eighth Cavalry, Fort Bliss, Texas, on September 15 and is stationed at Sierra Blanca, Texas, on October 19.

1916   Attached to Headquarters, Punitive Expedition into Mexico, March 13, and participates in the Rubio Ranch Affair, May 14. Promoted to first lieutenant, May 23.

1917   Promoted to captain, May 15. Sails for Europe on the *Baltic* with Pershing's staff as commanding officer. Assigned to Headquarters Troop, American Expeditionary Forces, May 28. Detailed to the Tank Service, November 10. Opens Light Tank Center and School in Langres, France, December 16.

1918   Promoted to major, January 23. Moves center and school to Bourg, France, February 22. Promoted to lieutenant colonel, April 3. Student, General Staff College, Langres, France, June 17. Organizes and commands the 1st Light Tank Brigade, August 24. Participates in St. Mihiel offensive, September 12–15. Wounded near Cheppy, France, in the Meuse-Argonne offensive, September 26. Promoted to colonel, October 17. Awarded Distinguished Service Cross, December 1.

1919   Sails for the United States, March 2. Arrives at Camp Meade in Maryland, March 25. Awarded Distinguished Service Medal, June 16.

1920   Reverted to regular grade of captain, June 30. Promoted to major, July 1. Joins the Third Cavalry, Fort Myer, Virginia, as commanding officer, Third Squadron, October 3.

1923   Attends Field Officers' Course, Fort Riley, Kansas, January 10. Attends Command and Staff College, Fort Leavenworth, Kansas, in September. Son George Smith Patton IV is born on December 24.

1924   Joins First Corps Headquarters, Boston, Massachusetts, as assistant chief of staff, G-1 (personnel), July 5.

1925   Joins Hawaiian Division as G-1 and G-2, March 31.

1928   Joins Office of Chief of Cavalry, Washington, D.C., May 7.

1931   Attends the Army War College, Washington, D.C.

1932   Joins the Third Cavalry, Fort Myer, Virginia, as executive officer, July 8.

1934   Promoted to lieutenant colonel, March 1.

1935   Joins the Hawaiian Department as G-2, June 8.

1937   Departs Honolulu, Hawaii, June 12. Hospitalized with a broken leg in Beverly, Massachusetts, July 25.

1938   Returns to duty status, February 2. Appointed executive officer, Academic Division at the Cavalry School and Ninth Cavalry,

Fort Riley, Kansas, February 8. Promoted to colonel, July 1.
Appointed commanding officer of the Fifth Cavalry, Fort
Clark, Texas, July 24. Appointed commanding officer of the
Third Cavalry, Fort Myer, Virginia, December 10.

1940   Appointed commanding officer of the 2nd Armored Brigade,
Second Armored Division, Fort Benning, Georgia, July 26.
Promoted to brigadier general, October 2. Named acting com-
manding general of the 2nd Armored Division, November 1.

1941   Promoted to major general, April 4. Participates in the
Tennessee, California, Louisiana, and Texas Maneuvers, June–
September.

1942   Appointed commanding general of the I Armored Corps,
January 15. Creates, organizes, and manages the Desert Train-
ing Center, March–July. Begins preparing for Operation
Torch, the invasion of French Northwest Africa, on July 30.
Invades French Morocco on November 8.

1943   Appointed commanding general of II Corps in Tunisia, March
6. Promoted to lieutenant general, March 12. Invades Sicily
as commanding general of the Seventh Army, July 10.

1944   Appointed commanding general of the Third Army, England,
January. The Third Army becomes operational in Normandy,
France, August 1.

1945   Promoted to general, April 14. Appointed commanding
general of the Fifteenth Army, October 6. Involved in an
automobile accident near Mannheim, Germany; hospitalized
in Heidelburg on December 9. Dies December 21. Interred
at Hamm, Luxembourg, December 24.

Family and Boyhood

The Pattons were aristocratic Virginians. Much as lords did in feudal times, they believed that their birth and family blood gave them the right to lead. They idealized their ancestors and sought to be like them in manners and achievement. Accepting the obligations of honor and responsibility, they were sure that they themselves were superior beings endowed with military virtues. Sixteen members of the Patton family fought for the Confederacy and all were heroes.[1] His forebears, Patton wrote, "have ever inspired me" to be "true to the heroic traditions of their race."[2]

Robert Patton, the first Patton in the New World, traveled from Scotland to Fredericksburg, Virginia, shortly before the American War of Independence. He was a successful merchant and, like many later Patton males, married well. In 1792 he took a wife, the daughter of Dr. Hugh Mercer, George Washington's friend and colleague and a brigadier general who had died in the Battle of Princeton.

One of Robert Patton's nine sons, John Mercer Patton, was a member of the Virginia legislature and, for a short time, an acting governor. Another of his sons, George Smith Patton, born in 1833, was General Patton's grandfather.

The first to bear the name George Smith, Patton's grandfather graduated from the Virginia Military Institute in 1852; practiced law in Charleston, now in West Virginia; and headed a volunteer militia company. He married Susan Thorton Glaswell, who bore him four children. The oldest was George William, General Patton's father. George was named after his father and two of his uncles who were both named William.

When the Civil War broke out in 1861, George Smith defended Charleston at the head of the Kanawha Riflemen. At Scary Creek, George's men stood toe-to-toe with Union soldiers, but when more Confederates moved up on his flank for reinforcement, George's men thought they were being outflanked by Yankee troops and began to retreat. Seeing their error, George rode his horse in front of the men and managed to turn some of them around. But just as he was restoring order to his line, a Union bullet caught his shoulder and dropped him off his horse. While he avoided the surgeon's saw by threatening the doctor with a pistol (which he wielded with his good hand), he ended up a prisoner of war when the bluecoats captured Charleston.

After a year of convalescence, George was paroled and returned to duty, where he resumed command of his unit. In May 1862 he led his men in the defense of southwest Virginia's rail lines. In one battle he was shot in the stomach, a wound that is almost always fatal. His commander found him propped up against a tree and writing a final letter to his wife. Thinking that George looked pretty healthy for a dying man, he examined the wound and dug out a gold coin that George's wife had given him. The bullet had bounced off the coin and did not penetrate his abdomen.

Returning to duty a third time after convalescing for blood poisoning, George was made the temporary commander of a cavalry brigade. He defeated a much larger Union force at Dry Creek, Virginia, near Lewisburg, in August. But the victory was followed by a defeat three months later at Droop Mountain, and George retreated south of Lewisburg. Continuing to fight and lead his men as the Confederacy began to disintegrate under the hammer blows of the Union army, George was felled again in the Third Battle of Winchester in September 1864. Once again in the saddle, George caught a chunk of shrapnel in his right hip while trying to rally his men. Brought to a house to recover, he threatened to kill anyone who tried to amputate his leg. But this time his luck did not hold out, and he died from infection six days later. According to family lore, the order promoting him to brigadier general, dispatched from Richmond, arrived shortly after his death.

During the war, Susan Thornton Glassell Patton, George's wife, was as dedicated as her husband to the Confederate cause. When she learned that her son George had befriended a Union sergeant who put his blue cap on the boy and told him he was now a Yankee, she scrubbed the child's head.[3] She also traveled to wherever her husband was convalescing to care for him. She had a sixth sense about her husband's woundings: her bags were already packed when the first two notices arrived. But when she received the third notice she packed slowly, telling friends she knew he would be dead before she arrived at his side.

Now a widow, Susan, who traced her lineage to relatives of George Washington, kings of England and France, and barons of Magna Carta fame, found herself with four young children in a devastated South. She accepted an invitation from her brother, Andrew Glassell, to join him in California and made the hazardous journey across the country to Los Angeles, where the family settled. To earn her living, she opened a private school. Life was difficult for a while, and General Patton's father "developed an intense aversion to poverty."[4]

In 1870 Susan Patton married George Hugh Smith, her first husband's cousin and schoolmate at VMI who had been badly wounded twice in the war. Smith had also been a colonel, commanding the 62nd and later the 25th Virginia Cavalry, and had gone to Mexico after the war but returned to Los Angeles to join Andrew Glassell's law firm. An expert on jurisprudence, he eventually became a judge of the southern California appellate court. The marriage produced two more children, a son who died as a child and a daughter named Ophelia.

So well did Smith raise his wife's children that the general's father changed his name from George William to George Smith Patton. The second to bear the name, he attended the Virginia Military Institute and was the first captain of the Corps of Cadets. He commanded the corps as they paraded at the Philadelphia Centennial Celebration Exhibition in 1876. It was the first appearance by Southern troops in the

North after the Civil War. After graduating in 1877, George stayed on for a year to teach French and then returned to Los Angeles to study law at Glassell and Smith. He became a member of the firm in 1880 and was later elected district attorney of Los Angeles County for two terms. In December 1884 he married Ruth Wilson, a daughter of Benjamin Davis Wilson.

The Wilsons were pioneers who personified the virtues of self-reliance. Physically strong and active, they were risk takers and among those who subdued the wilderness continent. They were straight shooters, hard workers, and self-made men and women. They participated in the rough and tumble life of the wild frontier.

Maj. David Wilson, a Pennsylvanian, served in the American War of Independence. He migrated to North Carolina and later to Tennessee, where he was elected Speaker of the House. His son, Benjamin Davis Wilson, was born in Nashville in 1811 and moved westward to open a trading post in Yazoo City, Mississippi. He continued to Santa Fe, where he became a trapper and Indian trader. He arrived in southern California in 1841, became a storekeeper, a rancher, and eventually a large landowner.

Wilson's life was filled with danger and excitement. He battled Indians, accepted a temporary commission in the U.S. Army, and was the first mayor of Los Angeles. A Yankee don—an American who had turned down Mexican leadership—Wilson founded the orange and citrus industry and planted the region's first vineyards. With Phineas Banning, a prominent Los Angeles businessman, he founded the town of Wilmington. Searching for timber for wine casks and orange crates, he cut a trail up what is now Mount Wilson; his burros later transported the first astronomical instruments to the hilltop's observatory. He bought an Army base after the Civil War and donated it to the Southern Methodist Church, which established Wilson College there. At San Gabriel he built the Church of Our Savior, the first Episcopal house of worship in southern California. He was elected to the state legislature twice. President Millard Fillmore appointed him as an Indian agent for southern California. Universally admired and respected, he owned more than fourteen thousand acres of land at his death.[5]

Wilson had married the daughter of a wealthy Mexican in 1844. They had a son who died as a young man and a daughter who would marry Wilson's secretary, De Barth Shorb. Mrs. Wilson died in 1849, and four years later, Wilson wed Margaret Short Hereford, a widow whose first husband had been a physician. The Wilsons had two daughters, Nannie and Ruth. Mr. Wilson died in 1877, and his former secretary and son-in-law, Shorb, took control of the Wilson interests. Shorb liked extravagant expenditures and eventually mortgaged the farm and the winery to continue his lifestyle.[6]

On December 10, 1884, Wilson's daughter Ruth wed George Smith Patton in the Church of Our Savior. The couple lived in the two-story adobe brick house built by Ruth's father in 1859 in what is now San Marino. Surrounding the residence, called Lake Vineyard, were hundreds of orange trees and thousands of raisin grape cuttings as well as olive, fig, pear, apple, apricot, nectarine, plum, cherry, almond, and walnut trees.[7] One year after her wedding, on November 11, 1885, at Lake Vineyard, Ruth gave birth to the future General Patton. She had a daughter, Anne, called Anita or Nita, two years later.

Soon after General Patton was born, he came down with the croup. Worried that the baby would die without being baptized, his nurse, a devout Irish Catholic woman, baptized him when no one else was in the room. The baby recovered from the illness and was baptized an Episcopalian. In later life, Patton preferred to have Catholic priests serving as chaplains in his armies; he considered them militant to his liking.[8]

George Smith Patton, the third to bear this name and who would be known as Junior, adored his father. As a child, when he said good night, he gave his mother only a single kiss but showered his father with kisses. He paid little attention to the Wilson side of his heritage, never realizing how much he resembled his maternal grandfather. Georgie, as he was known to his family, played soldier, learned to ride and shoot at an early age, fished, swam, hunted, sailed boats, and generally lived the outdoor life. He had a carpenter shop and—from Phineas Banning's son Capt. William Banning—a set of tools. He had a table for ping-pong as well as horses, a dog, swords, and a shotgun. In the evenings his father or Aunt Nannie would read Bible stories, Scottish legends, Shakespeare plays, and Kipling poetry to Georgie and his sister. When Georgie was about seven years old, his father read the *Iliad* and the

Odyssey to him and Nita. The father would sit in the big chair near the fireplace, one child in his lap, the other cuddled beside him. "I must be the happiest boy in the world," Georgie once wrote.[9]

The Civil War was a strong influence on young Georgie. He prayed every night to a painting he thought was of God and Jesus Christ. Only when he was older did he learn the two bearded men were Robert E. Lee and Stonewall Jackson. His father told him stories about the war and drew morality tales from the heroism of Jackson and the Pattons who died in the war.[10] One such story involved his great grandmother, Peggy, who attended church with Patton's father while he was attending VMI. After church, an ex-Confederate colonel rode by on his horse. Peggy asked him if he said "amen" when the minister asked for the congregation to pray for the president and all those in authority. He said that he had and added, "The war is over, after all." Peggy lashed him across his face with her buggy whip before telling Patton's father to "drive on!"[11]

Young Georgie was also influenced Col. John Singleton Mosby, the famous (and infamous) Confederate guerrilla leader. Mosby, employed by the Southern Pacific Railroad, became a friend of the Patton family and entertained young Georgie with exciting tales of his war exploits. Georgie could not get enough Civil War stories. Once he and his sister exchanged clothes before dinner as a lark, and during the meal, the elder Patton began telling stories about Robert E. Lee at the table. When little Georgie became excited, his father reprimanded him for enjoying a war story in girl's clothing. Little George cried.[12]

Aunt Nannie was also a heavy influence in the young boy's life. A spinster, Nannie made little secret of her love for Georgie's father (she even tried to accompany her sister and her new husband on their honeymoon). She lived with the family as surrogate parent to the children, but her focus was on Georgie. Because she could not have George Sr., she devoted her life to George Jr. Accordingly, she praised anything the boy did and would not allow criticism of him, for she said he was "delicate."

At age seven, after abandoning his desire to become a fireman, Georgie decided to become a soldier. He feared that he would get "the call" from God to be a priest and prayed every night that Jesus would spare him so he could fulfill his destiny as a soldier.[13] His father encouraged him, giving him toy soldiers, play swords, and a soldier's uniform, which he used to their fullest potential.[14] Once Georgie tried unsuccessfully to get his sister to reenact a scene from the *Iliad* in which he would tie her with a rope and drag her behind his pony as a dead Trojan. In reenacting a battle tactic from the campaigns of John the Blind of Bohemia, Georgie and his cousins wheeled a wagon up a hill over the family's turkey shed. Then, at Georgie's command, they rolled down the hill, throwing sticks as spears. The wagon crashed through a fence and left more than one dead turkey in its path. The mini-blitzkrieg exercise ended when Georgie's mother ran outside, demanding an explanation. Georgie told her about John the Blind, and she asked him how he knew about him. Georgie shrugged and explained, "Oh, I was there."[15]

Mr. Patton invested in ventures with Phineas Banning's three sons, Hancock, William, and Joseph, who owned carriages and maintained transportation lines. In 1892 Patton also invested with the Bannings in the purchase of Santa Catalina Island, twenty-six miles off Los Angeles's shore, where the Patton family vacationed. Little Georgie spent many a day there, playing and hunting. He and Nita went to parties and danced at the pavilion.

When De Barth Shorb died in 1896 and it was discovered he had been running the Wilson farm into huge debts, Mr. Patton went to work to keep the farm out of foreclosure and make it profitable again. Fearful of the kind of poverty he experienced as a young boy during the Civil War, he made it his goal to keep the family from facing the same hardships. With a newfound energy at age forty, he dedicated almost all of his time to saving the family's resources, denying his son the intense attention he had given before. Georgie resented the shift of attention and harbored a resentment toward his spendthrift uncle for the rest of his life.

Mr. Patton ran for the U.S. Congress twice as a Democrat, in 1894 and 1896, and lost both times. Georgie did not like the idea of his father as a congressman. He and Nita openly rooted for his opponent in the first election, "as we hated the thought of leaving home," and Georgie was unenthusiastic about the second race, hoping that if his father lost he would once again become the object of his attention. The family's financial problems put an end to any such return to earlier days.[16]

Whether Georgie was dyslexic or had what is now called "attention deficit disorder" (ADD) has been debated. Only the most circumstantial evidence exists for either scenario. His parents waited until he was eleven years old to send him to school. His spelling was quaint, often comical, and a problem throughout his life. At the Virginia Military Institute, after Georgie failed to understand a written order posted for all cadets, his father told him to read all such announcements at least three times to be sure he understood what was written. At West Point, his worries, doubts, and poor estimate of himself bespoke what is now called attention deficit disorder. Later in life he outgrew his earlier symptoms, read a great deal, and wrote poetry, articles, and two book-length manuscripts, although his spelling was still poor. Dyslexia and ADD have a side effect: their sufferers have to work twice as hard to understand half as much. Thus Patton forced himself to memorize ancient texts, bible stories, and later, his textbooks.

Two months shy of his twelfth birthday, Georgie's parents, over his Aunt Nannie's protests, decided he needed formal schooling. At Stephen Cutter Clark's Classical School for Boys, from 1897 to 1903, Patton gained the rudiments of a high school education. It was hard at first, when he realized he was the only boy who could not read or write. His pampered, isolated upbringing had not prepared him to compete with other children his age. But he adjusted. Once he learned how to read, he poured over his books, memorizing them.

His best subject was history, particularly ancient history, which contained a large measure of wars, campaigns, and conquests and which demonstrated the consequences of moral decisions made by good or bad men. Very quickly he chose his favorite historical figures—Alexander the Great, "who always aspired to perfection in everything"; Julius Caesar, whose "system of intelligence . . . was excellent"; and Epaminondas, who "had the best character of all the famous Greeks . . . almost a perfect man." Cleon, on the other hand, "was a great baster [*sic*]."[17]

The compositions Georgie wrote contained several persistent themes: gaining credit and recognition, achieving fame and glory through heroism, and enjoying physical comfort and pleasure. He had a flair for writing, and soon after entering school, he began writing letters to relatives.[18]

Georgie's father continued to encourage his son's interest in a military career, possibly out of his own regret for never having served. When the Spanish-American War broke out in 1898, he told Georgie that he had been offered a colonel's rank and would take the boy with him to go on the campaign. Georgie was excited by the prospect of seeing combat, but nothing came of his father's boast. For all his stories of glory on the battlefield and of Patton forefathers dying at the head of their men in battle, George Sr. was not a warrior. Once, when the two were hunting wild goats, Georgie asked his father why he never carried a gun on their hunts or a fishing rod when they went fishing. "I am a man of peace," his father explained apologetically.[19]

In 1902 Frederick Ayer, a very wealthy eighty-year-old man; his wife, Ellen Barrows Banning Ayer; and their children Beatrice, Katherine, and Frederick Jr. traveled from Massachusetts to visit the Bannings of California. The families stayed at Santa Catalina Island, where the Pattons were also spending the summer. Georgie, almost seventeen years old, and Beatrice, aged sixteen, met that summer. They participated in a play featuring the Ayer, Banning, and Patton cousins put on in Joseph Banning's house. A Los Angeles newspaper society reporter covered the occasion.[20]

Patton was not immediately smitten with Beatrice. He thought her too young to be seen with him around Catalina Island. The fact that she carried a doll did not help to disguise her youth. Beatrice, however, was an impressive young lady. She spoke fluent French—in fact, she earned the doll she carried by speaking only French for three months. She was considered the Belle of Boston and had already turned down three marriage proposals. She had been to Europe and Egypt, whereas Georgie had never been outside the United States. She could be as capricious as Georgie too. While in Egypt she had snapped the toe of a mummy, to take as a souvenir, while exploring a newly opened tomb. She also attempted to get a tattoo but was caught by her governess before she could get it inked onto her chest. Eventually, Georgie and Bea became friends, and after the Ayers returned home, they corresponded somewhat self-consciously from time to time.[21]

Meanwhile, in that year, Georgie had begun to take serious steps toward becoming a soldier. To become a regular officer, a commission from the U.S. Military Academy at West Point was required. Gaining admission to West Point was difficult, for the student body was small. Georgie's father wrote to Republican senator Thomas R. Barb of California starting his quest for his son's appointment. He learned that Barb did not have an appointment available for two years, when the cadet he sponsored would graduate. Thus Patton asked his friend Judge Harry T. Lee, a Republican, for help. Lee had been a major in the Union forces during the Civil War and had seen a brave Patton fall at the battle of Gettysburg. Lee wrote a strong letter of recommendation to Barb and cited Georgie's "fighting stock"—Mercer, the grandfather Patton, and "the late Hon. B.D. Wilson."[22]

Georgie had a firm wish to be a regular Army officer, and so the alternatives to West Point—including the Virginia Military Institute, where his father had friends and relatives in the administration, and the University of Arizona, where his cousin was the commander of cadets—would not do. Mr. Patton wrote a follow-up letter to Senator Barb, stressing his Georgie's military background, his "heredity . . . strains of blood," as well as his excellent health and morality.[23] Barb replied that Georgie would have to compete fairly with the other candidates. He could take an examination for admission at the senator's office in California.

Aware of Georgie's poor spelling and his general lack of book learning, Mr. Patton decided to continue to apply his influence. A member of the California Club, he called upon his friends who were leading businessmen and political figures to send letters to Barb. He also asked his stepfather, Colonel Smith, to write. Missives poured in on Barb, who was impressed but insisted that all the young men who were interested in the appointment had to take the exam.

Princeton University and the Morristown Prep School accepted Georgie in the fall of 1903, but Mr. Patton by then had decided to send Georgie to the Virginia Military Institute. Gaining admission to VMI was easy, for two generations of Pattons had preceded him. The decision made great sense. If Georgie received Barb's appointment, he would have a year of preparation for his studies at West Point and time to accustom himself to living away from home. If he failed to obtain the appointment, he could continue at VMI, where honor graduates sometimes received regular Army commissions.

Georgie's parents took him east to enroll at VMI that summer. While in Lexington, they stayed with relatives. One day when walking with his uncle Glassell Patton, Georgie mentioned his fear of being "cowardly." His uncle replied that "no Patton could be a coward" because all Pattons were "most recklessly brave." Georgie told his father about the conversation, and his father further assured him that his "breeding made him perfectly willing to face death from weapons with a smile." Young Patton was convinced. "I think," he wrote, "that this is true."[24] Still, his potential for cowardice would torment him for the rest of his life.

2

Virginia Military Institute and West Point

W hen Patton entered the Virginia Military Institute in 1903, the cadet first captain told his father, "Of course you realize, Mr. Patton, that your son is a cadet and cannot leave the grounds." His father, however, could and did leave campus. George never felt so alone.[1] But when he went to get measured for his uniform, the elderly tailor noted that his size was exactly the same as that of his father and grandfather. He felt at once that he was home.

His letters to his mother and sister, Nita, who took over his mother's duties during George's second semester, were typical of any first-year college student. They were full of requests for clothes, food, and grooming items, and they were almost insolent. They lacked the word "please" and often began with "Send me. . . ." George chastised his mother and Nita for sending him candy, which he liked but which made him gain weight. He wanted more uniforms, which he would change up to ten times a day to look sharp. He also needed hair tonic to fight his receding hairline. Although he received the tonic, he could see that it was not working. "I shall need a wig," he wrote.[2]

His father had offered Georgie advice on how to comport himself at VMI. "Be nice and appreciate when the older cadets notice you," Papa had said, "but hold yourself aloof and do not seek their society." The best course was to "Make your friends among your own classmates." Finally, "be a good soldier first," then be a good scholar.[3] In other words, polish your brass before you hit the books. Young Patton followed these precepts and had a wonderful time. He was in Patton country. Not only had his father and grandfather attended VMI, but six of his great uncles had been educated there. The Lexington cemetery was filled with Pattons, other relatives, and family friends. "I have so many kinfolk here," he once wrote his father, "that when I am not walking on them, I'm kissing them." He enjoyed his schoolmates, received good grades in his courses, joined a secret fraternity, sent a silk VMI flag to Beatrice for Christmas, and prodded his father to get him appointed to West Point.[4]

Senator Barb's announcement of the time and place for his examination for West Point candidates—mid-February 1904 in Los Angeles—was a bombshell for the Patton family. To avoid a transcontinental voyage from VMI to California as well as a long furlough and absence from classes, Georgie's father asked if the boy could take the exam in Washington. Bard's answer was negative. Georgie's "general standing" at VMI was excellent: of ninety-three fourth-class students, he was ninth in mathematics, tenth in Latin, second in history, and sixth in drawing, and he had received no demerits since his arrival. Thus, the trip to the West Coast for the exam hardly seemed worthwhile. Did Georgie really want to go to West Point? The answer was yes. A flurry of letters and telegrams passed between Mr. Patton and a variety of people involved—not only Senator Bard but also various cousins, classmates, and friends of the VMI faculty and staff. If Georgie passed the test, he wanted everything in place to push his nomination.

Georgie finished his first semester's studies at VMI and spent Christmas Day eating figs at Stonewall Jackson's tombstone. He liked spending time in cemeteries and on battlefields where his ancestors fought, trying to soak up the history and connect with the past. Once, on a trip to Gettysburg, he wandered through the battlefield cemetery to "let the spirits of the dead thousands . . . sink deep into me." He then wandered over to the site of Pickett's charge and sat down on a rock near where two of his great uncles had died. As the sun went down he "drank it all in till I was quite happy."[5]

In February Georgie took the train west, studying history, geography, and spelling on the way. He took the West Point exam with fifteen other candidates on February 15, 1904, at the Hotel Van Nuys on Broadway. On the following day, he took the train back east. The Los Angeles newspapers carried the recommendations of the examining committee, a group of prominent Los Angeles citizens, among them Judge Harry Lee, Mr. Patton's friend. They sent the names of the three young men who had passed, Patton's among them, to Senator Barb. Immediately thereafter, a deluge of letters from well-known residents of Los Angeles urged Barb to select Patton for sponsorship.

Barb took until March 3 to make up his mind. He sent a telegram to Mr. Patton with the good news. He was appointing Georgie. "Dear Papa," Georgie wrote when he learned of the senator's action, "well, I guess I have got it. And I am beastly glad and am sure you are. As for Mr. Barb, I rank him and the pope on an equal plane of hollyness [sic]."[6] Several days later, Georgie wrote another letter, expressing more fully his sentiments. He concluded, "Well everything is now settled. And with the help of God and a vigorous use of your influence I have the appointment. Your loving and grateful son."[7]

Early in May, Patton traveled to Fort McHenry in Baltimore with two schoolmates for a physical examination, which he passed. Three weeks later the War Department notified him he had met the requirements for admission to the U.S. Military Academy. He was to report on June 16, 1904, between 8:00 a.m. and noon.

Before Patton left VMI, the commander of cadets informed him that, had he stayed, he would have been appointed the first corporal of his class, the highest military honor. Had he remained at the school for four years, he would, no doubt, have maintained a distinctive academic and military record without great effort. He probably would have gained a regular commission.

Patton's single year in Virginia reinforced in him his Southern roots and the Patton heritage. Now he would break two generations of tradition, go north, enter a college with more difficult courses, and compete with students who came from all over the country. The way was fraught with challenges. Mr. Patton accompanied Georgie to West Point the day before he was to report. As they walked around the campus, Georgie noted, "all the cadets saluted [his father] thinking from his bearing that he must be an officer."[8]

He found West Point, he told his mother, "pretty nice." He was treated "a lot better than at V.M.I." The upperclassmen did not touch the plebes or "sware." Everyone had to take a bath every night and shave every day. The food was "fine" with "lots of variety" and "dessert twice a day." The tablecloths were changed every day.[9]

Shortly after his arrival, Georgie attended a Fourth of July celebration and listened to an oration about the modern soldier. The speech set him thinking, and he soon realized he disagreed with the point of view expressed. He was different from the cadets at VMI and West Point, he wrote to his father, for he belonged to "a class perhaps almost extinct," that is, a category "as far removed from those lazy, patriotic, or peace soldiers as heaven is from hell." Unlike them, Patton was ambitious—supremely so—and he would do his best to attain what he considered to be his destiny.[10] This letter was the first in which he invoked his destiny or fate. In his subsequent correspondence and journal entries, it became clear he felt strongly that he was destined to accomplish something out of the ordinary, something grand and honorable, perhaps a high rank or a spectacular achievement in battle.

As he thought increasingly about his future, he began to harden his exterior, to work toward showing a warrior face, to stifle emotion, and to seek a machinelike perfection in all things military. He wrote his father, "I would like to get killed in a great victory," and then have his body "born between the ranks of my defeated enemy and his spirit descending and hearing the compliments of people." His machinelike perfection appeared when the cadets walked in small groups to classes and to meals. The group leaders rotated commands, and when Patton led the cadets, the men in ranks always marched in unison, something he felt only he could achieve. Sometimes, though not often, Patton "crawled," or punished, them. He said, "When I get in front of them, the foolishness stops."[11]

Patton loved "Beast Barracks," the period during the summer of his entrance when the cadets lived in tents and were taught military activities: how to stand, march, salute, and be a soldier. He hated the fall and the impending academic work. Following his father's advice at VMI,

Patton first perfected his appearance and dress, ironing his trousers more than necessary, before looking at his books. As a result, he was less than brilliant in his studies, although he ranked in the middle of the class. The work was much more difficult than it had been at VMI.

Patton tolerated his two roommates more than he bonded with them. They were hardworking, middle-class men, and they kept clean, he wrote, but they were not gentlemen. Either way, he would continue to room with them until he found "some other fellows who were gentlemen." Patton's arrogance came from years of cultivation under his father. Constantly reminded of his family's bravery, breeding, and greatness, he viewed anyone from outside his world of Southern gentlemen and honorable soldiers as somewhat beneath him. Patton's father became his main pen pal. Georgie would write to him about everything, and his father would offer advice, counsel, and encouragement.

While he was at West Point, the Ayer family invited the young cadet to their Boston home whenever he could get off campus. When there, "we ride, swim, sail, motor and see *Bee.*" Over time, his feelings for Beatrice deepened. He admitted as much to his mother when he wrote to tell her, "She is the only girl I have ever loved. . . . Gosh, those skirted bipeds at Catalina, who pawn themselves off as girls, aren't in it with her shadow."[12] Patton's correspondence with Beatrice became regular and increasingly personal. At first the letters were banal, but gradually he began sharing his innermost thoughts with her—his feelings of inferiority, his apparent inability to study, his small failures and large doubts. She seemed to understand him, and she buoyed him, bringing him out of his near depression and disappointment.

His symptoms of dyslexia or attention deficit disorder contributed to these feelings of inferiority and his inattention to his studies, and he needed constant encouragement from his parents and from Beatrice. He wrote often of "my stupidity." "I have gotten so I don't care whether I amount to anything or not," he wrote his father, "but am trying to over-come this somnistic condition and work." A week later, he wrote, "I said I had lost the capacity for running [studying]. Well the mere expression of that thought in writing seemed to dissipate it for ever since then I have been running with my usual eagerness."

Then his usual self-deprecation took hold. "I have ideals without strength of character enough to live up to them and they [the other cadets] have not even got them [the ideals]," he told his father. To Beatrice, he wrote that he was "oppressed with the knowledge of how little I have done [in life]; it makes me feel worthless." No one had tried so hard to be first in everything only to fail utterly. "I have lived 19 years," he told Papa, "yet it seems to me that I have wasted them. I amount to very little." "I am either very lazy or very stupid or both."[13]

By the spring of 1905, Patton was aware that his efforts to be military and studious were making him feel deficient. "It is exasperating," he told his father, "to see a lot of fools who don't care beat you out when you work hard. . . . I can't think of any thing but my own worthlessness."[14]

Patton's grades suffered. At the end of his first year at the Point, Patton was required to take several makeup exams. He ultimately failed French and mathematics. Ordinarily he would have been asked to resign, but the authorities were impressed with his military aptitude and his constant struggle to do his best. They decided to have him repeat his plebe, or first, year at the academy. Neither Papa nor Mama "ever showed by word or deed their disappointment at my failure," he wrote many years afterward.[15] They understood that he had tried to do his best. He resented being a "rat," or first-year man, again. It would mean being a freshman for a third year in a row. It confirmed all his fears about his perceived lack of intelligence. He had not been this stunned and ashamed of his inabilities since he had entered Stephen Cutter Clark's School for Boys five years earlier.[16]

He spent the summer with his family on Santa Catalina Island to recover his spirits. He went horseback riding and took a nasty fall, the first in a series of riding injuries.[17] He also started a notebook in which he wrote his most serious thoughts. The first entry was "Do your damdest always." Other notations were: "Always do more than is required of you." "Do everything to attract attention. . . . Do all you can not only all you have to do . . . No sacrifice is too great if by it you can attain an end."

"Tactics," he wrote, "is strategy in minatured and the essence of both is speed." "Always work like Hell at all things at all times." "You must of yourself merit and obtain . . . applause by your own efforts." "Never Never Never stop being ambitious."[18]

Patton returned to West Point in 1905 as a plebe, but since he was repeating the year, he did not have to go through the hazing the other "rats" had to endure. He was better adjusted to the academy's standards and found his studying paid off with better grades. He also began to write poetry. His biggest thrill of the second year came when the West Point football team played Princeton. President Theodore Roosevelt attended the game and Patton was picked to be one of his escorts: "I nearly burst."[19]

Patton went out for the football team but never made varsity. In practice scrimmages, he played so fiercely that he suffered broken bones, bruises, strained muscles, and sprains. After being treated for an injured arm, he wrote Bea that the injury was actually a blessing in disguise because it had "probably saved me from breaking my neck." Patton also participated in other activities on campus. He became proficient at the broadsword and spent many hours fencing. In his junior year, at the annual Field Day, he won the 220-yard hurdles, breaking the school record. He finished second in the 220-yard dash. He was a star in polo, and he easily gained his athletic letter "A" for Army.

He passed his examinations that year, although he worried about his grades and standing from time to time. In his second year, he was named second corporal, a great accomplishment for him. But his first taste of authority was almost too much for a cadet who had been on the receiving end for three years. He seemed to anger everyone: the plebes, his classmates, and even the tactical officers. He gave more demerits than any other upperclassman. Despite his overzealousness, he found that abusing plebes did not amuse him "as I had hoped." His draconian methods soon began to overwhelm him. He became angry at just the sight of plebes and, at one point, stayed angry for three straight days. His behavior was noticed and he was soon reduced to sixth corporal.[20]

Later he was promoted again to second corporal and then sergeant major. In his senior year, he was named adjutant, the second-highest cadet rank, but the one he really wanted. As adjutant he read the daily orders and was out in front of the cadet parade formation. He loved the position.

"I have always fancied myself a coward," he wrote his father. But no longer did he think so. While at the firing range one day in his senior year, Patton took his turn to work in the pits, raising, lowering, and marking the targets. Suddenly, while the cadets were firing, Patton stood erect to test his courage under fire. It was almost a miracle that he was not hit or killed.

To Bea he wrote that three things in life were important to him: heredity, love of excitement, and desire for reputation. Nothing else was worthwhile. "I don't want pleasure," he told her, "I want success." To his father he wrote, "I am still an ass."

He invited Bea to dances and football games at West Point and gloried in her company. She in turn was impressed with his military bearing. After watching him on the parade grounds, putting younger cadets though their drills, she wrote his parents that he "seemed by far the most military person on the post that day; our only anxiety was that he might break in two at the waistline."[21]

Patton visited Beatrice during his senior year Christmas break. He had a great time, as usual, and planned to steal a kiss and propose marriage. He was nervous and worried about her response to his kiss, let alone his proposal. When he found himself alone with her in the Ayer library, he likened the anticipation of the kiss to "pointing a gun at yourself and pulling the trigger in order to prove it is not loaded and it is not particularly enjoyable especially when you think it is loaded." He need not have worried; she responded in kind. For his marriage proposal, he had a clever exit plan in case she said no. In his pocket he kept a fake telegram, which ordered him to return immediately to West Point. Again, his worries were for naught. Although surprised by his proposal, she said yes.[22]

In January of his senior year, he wrote to Bea's father to thank him for the Christmas vacation he had spent with the Ayer family "and to explain myself." He had "loved Beatrice ever since the summer in California," and he had finally told her so on the previous December 30. Even though she had accepted his marriage proposal, he had "asked nothing in return," for he understood how Mr. Ayer regarded the military profession—as "narrowing in tendency." Yet Patton admitted that he was "only capable of being a soldier," and so the matter rested for the moment.[23]

As graduation approached, he had to choose his branch of service. Because his general standing was not high enough to enter the Engineer Corps, his options were the infantry, cavalry, and artillery. There seemed to be more promotions in the infantry, but he listened to Capt. Charles Summerall, then a senior instructor, later a division and corps commander in World War I, and, finally, U.S. chief of staff. Summerall encouraged Patton to be a cavalryman. Although promotions were slow, the branch reorganized and promoted officers who were not only good in their jobs but also proficient in their abilities. Patton chose the cavalry.

Graduating in June 1909, Patton stood number 46 of 103 graduates, among them, John H. C. Lee, Jacob Devers, Robert Eichelberger, Edwin Forrest Harding, and William H. Simpson, all of whom were destined to attain high rank and distinction in World War II. The newly graduated and commissioned second lieutenants celebrated at their class banquet at the Hotel Astor in New York City. On the following day, George's parents bought him an expensive watch at Tiffany's.

Patton's classmates regarded him with admiration for his fairness, with condescension for his naïve earnestness, and with discomfort for his obsession for future glory. He had no close friends but was devoted to duty, honor, and country; to order and discipline; to the spirit of West Point; and to the idea of "can do."

In the spring of 1909, several weeks before graduation, he was already thinking about how he could get assigned to Washington, D.C., where the important people were.

3

Mexico and World War I

T he new lieutenant was first assigned to Fort Sheridan near
Chicago and was eager to learn the rudiments of soldiering. Although
he had arrived at the post with his usual nervousness in the form of hay
fever, he was soon comfortable with his abilities, his colleagues, and the
customs of the service. His superiors were helpful. He fulfilled his tasks,
as always, seriously, hoping to impress with his willingness and hard
work. Yet he had to prove himself, and so he entered into many extra-
curricular activities. He rode to the hounds, set up a polo field, coached
a football team, and inaugurated a study of military leadership. He also
maintained an extensive social life, dating several girls in the wealthy
suburban counties, taking them to dances, parties, and the theater.

Despite his active social life, his heart belonged to Bea. He exchanged
more letters with her father, defending his choice to stay in the military
and his desire to marry her. Mr. Ayer did not like the idea of his daughter living the Army life, being transferred from base to base, in squalid
living conditions. He also wanted to visit his daughter at will, while the
Army could move her to another country at its whim. The stress of Mr.
Ayer's stubbornness caused Patton to lose weight and stay up nights
worrying. He could not believe the love of his life was interfering with
his destiny as a soldier.[1]

Patton's persistence paid off. Mr. Ayer consented to the marriage after a month of correspondence, asking him to keep "ever in mind" the family's desire to see Beatrice from time to time. Later, he wrote George another letter, telling him that he, Mr. Ayer, would earn the money and George would earn the glory. George was not the only one who was persistent. Beatrice had locked herself in her room and went on a hunger strike for a week until her father gave in (food snuck in to her by her mother and siblings helped her resolve).[2] As it turned out, she may have gotten more than she bargained for. On her first trip to Fort Sheridan, she offered to break the engagement, doubting that she could make a good Army wife. Exacerbating her experience was the fact that George had taken the worst living quarters on the base, to avoid being bumped from nicer quarters by a higher-ranking officer, who, by Army tradition, had the right to "rank out" a lower-ranking officer from the place he preferred. George reassured Beatrice with kisses.[3]

Two events out of the ordinary launched the Patton legend. In the stables one afternoon, Patton noticed a horse untied. He berated the responsible soldier, ordered him to run to the animal, correct the oversight, and run back. Instead of running, the culprit walked at a rapid gait. "Run, damn you, run!" Patton shouted, losing his temper. The man obeyed. Later, reflecting on the insult he had laid on the soldier by damning him, Patton called together all the men in the stable and apologized to the man in front of the group. A public apology by an officer to an enlisted man was unheard of, and the troops in the barracks wondered what sort of officer Patton was. Was he a nut? Or was he just sensitive to human beings, even enlisted men, and fair in his dealings with them?[4]

The second incident occurred while Patton, on horseback, was drilling some troops. His horse bucked unexpectedly and threw Patton, who immediately remounted. Once again the animal bucked, then reared, and fell. When the horse stood, Patton was still in the saddle. The beast threw his head back and struck Patton on the forehead, opening a gash on his eyebrow. Unaware that he was bleeding until he saw blood running down his sleeve, he continued to drill his soldiers for about twenty minutes. After dismissing the men, he washed his face at troop headquarters, taught a scheduled class of noncommissioned officers, and attended a class for junior officers. Only then did he see a doctor to stitch his injury. The enlisted men were impressed. Here was an officer who would lead even when he was injured. The men embellished the story as it made the rounds in the barracks.[5]

In May 1910, Patton married Beatrice Ayer in a high society wedding in Massachusetts. It was the first military wedding on the state's North Shore since the Civil War. George's mother fell ill and could not attend, so Aunt Nannie stood in her place and remained on her nephew's arm during the reception. It was her dream come true—never mind that the local newspaper failed to describe her dress.[6]

During the honeymoon in England, Patton bought a copy of Karl von Clausewitz's *On War*. When they returned from overseas, Beatrice became pregnant. They settled into normal military life, waiting for their first child. Now ready to begin his professional career, one desire tortured Patton. "Beaty," he said, "we must amount to something."[7]

The birth of their daughter, Beatrice Jr., in March 1911 was a wrenching experience for Patton. He witnessed the event, but when someone handed him the newborn, he rushed from the room and threw up in the kitchen sink.[8] With the baby taking much of his wife's attention, Patton bought a typewriter and began writing about military topics. His persistent theme was his belief in the attack. Furthermore, he wrote, the effectiveness of a machine or a weapon was only as good as the person using it. Thus training and discipline were essential.[9]

Patton continued to test his courage, but this time he met unexpected results. Again, he returned to his old West Point practice of sticking his head up at the far end of the rifle range. The routine reinforced his belief in his own bravery, but one afternoon when he returned home, he found Bea with her bags packed and the baby in her arms, waiting for a taxi to take her to Chicago. An officer's wife had reported the practice to her and asked if the couple was having marital difficulties. Patton was forced to explain his real motives. She agreed to unpack but was not amused.[10]

While at Fort Sheridan, Patton bought an automobile and loved driving it as much as he loved tinkering with its engine. It was the start of his interest in the internal combustion engine, and this interest would prove to be important in the combat he would see later. He also took temporary command of a machine-gun platoon, which he thought was a poor outfit, but the experience, too, would prove invaluable.[11]

In pursuit of his ambitions to be "somebody" and noticed favorably, Patton pulled strings and was transferred in December 1911 to Fort Myer, Virginia, across the Potomac River from Washington D.C., "a place," Patton said, "where all people with aspirations should hope to dwell." While riding his horse one day along one of the fort's equestrian trails, he came across another rider, Secretary of War Henry Stimson. The two rode together and quickly developed a friendship that would last the rest of Patton's life and come in handy later when Patton's career hit a crisis.[12] Patton quickly became a member of Washington's elite and was well known in military circles, including the Army chief of staff.

Selected to represent the United States in the 1912 Olympics at Stockholm, Sweden, Patton competed in the modern pentathlon, which included a pistol shoot, the three-hundred-meter swim, fencing, a steeple-chase ride, and a two-and-a-half-mile run. Patton pushed himself mercilessly as he began training. He went on a diet of raw meat and salad and gave up smoking and alcohol. On the liner to Europe with Beatrice, he dueled with his fellow Olympiads, ran laps around the deck, and swam in a tank with a rope holding him in position.

At the games, Patton fired well on his first day of the pistol shoot, but on the second, two bullets apparently missed the target, launching the myth that his aim was so good that the two bullets passed through holes made by his previous bullets. The judges did not see it that way and penalized him ten points. He came in sixth in the swim but pushed himself so hard that he had to be helped from the pool with a boathook. He finished third in fencing and handed the French fencer, a world-class competitor, his only defeat. He had a perfect score in the steeple-chase but came in third behind two other contestants who had faster times. During the two-and-a-half mile run, Patton drove himself hard, without pacing, so that he entered the stadium first, but slowed to a walk as two runners passed him. He walked across the finish line and collapsed. Overall, he finished fifth out of forty-two.

After the Olympics, the Pattons and Ayers (both families attended the games) visited Berlin, Dresden, and Nuremberg. Patton and Beatrice traveled to Saumur, France, the site of the cavalry school. For two weeks

Patton studied fencing with the European champion. Patton and his teacher developed a close relationship, and Patton vowed to return someday and complete his training.

On his return to Fort Myer, Patton opened a campaign to change the sword used by the U.S. Army. Since before the Civil War, the Army had used a curved sword. Patton advocated a straight one, like the one used by the French army. The straight sword was better for the attack, Patton argued in several articles, and enabled cavalrymen to maintain their speed, while a curved sword slowed the cavalryman, who had to swing against the momentum of his horse. Patton's ideas gained prominence. In 1913 the secretary of war ordered a new, straight sword forged for the Army. It was known as the Patton sword.

That summer, Patton returned to Saumur, France, this time on War Department orders to perfect his swordsmanship. He worked hard for six weeks. In addition, he learned to speak passable French. Patton and Beatrice spent his off hours driving around the countryside, studying Caesar's and Attila the Hun's battle sites "for the next time around." Patton swore he had fought here before and that he would fight here again and told his wife so.[13]

Named Master of the Sword, Patton's next assignment was to Fort Riley, Kansas, to teach swordsmanship, write new regulations for the cavalry, and take the advanced courses at the Cavalry School. The outbreak of World War I prompted Patton to think of resigning his commission and joining the French army. Gen. Leonard Wood, a friend who had been Army chief of staff, discouraged him from doing so.

Leery that his cavalry regiment was scheduled for service in the Philippines, far from the conflict in Europe, Patton again pulled strings and received a transfer to a regiment at Fort Bliss in El Paso, Texas, where Brig. Gen. John J. Pershing commanded. Beatrice became pregnant again and gave birth to their second daughter, Ruth Ellen, so named even though Patton wanted to name her Beatrice Second "like a racehorse."[14] His sister, Nita, came for a visit and fell in love with the widower Pershing.

On March 9, 1916, the Mexican bandit Pancho Villa crossed the border and raided the town of Columbus, New Mexico, killing sixteen Americans. President Woodrow Wilson ordered Pershing to form an expedition to pursue Villa and bring him to justice. When Patton realized he would not be included in the venture, he obtained permission to speak to Pershing. He implored Pershing to take him along, and Pershing retorted, "Everyone wants to go, why should I favor you?" Without missing a beat, Patton replied, "Because I want to go more than anyone else." Patton's heartfelt argument swayed the commander, and Pershing appointed him as one of his aides.[15]

The Punitive Expedition consisted of roughly forty-eight hundred men, some on horseback, others riding in trucks and cars. Kicking off on March 16, a mere seven days after Villa's attack, it was the first expedition in which the U.S. Army used motorized vehicles. Despite the initial excitement of a wartime commitment, the campaign turned out to be long and fruitless. Although the troops traveled four hundred miles into Mexico, Pershing's men never found Villa. But Patton proved himself to be a hero anyhow.[16]

Patton was sent to find corn in the town of Rubio with ten soldiers and four civilians traveling in three cars. During the foray, one of Patton's scouts recognized several Villistas at a nearby ranch. Taking advantage of his mobility and speed, Patton quickly organized a plan of attack. He had the three cars race for the ranch and stop at its southern edge while Patton stopped at the northern edge. With the ranch somewhat surrounded, the men then dismounted and closed on the house. Patton, armed with a rifle and pistol, watched as three men on horseback bolted out of the house. They headed south, but seeing the Americans, turned and charged Patton. They opened fire, kicking up gravel in front of him. Realizing these men were not civilians but Villa's men, Patton fired five shots from his pistol, killing one of the horses and breaking one of the rider's arms. With his men running up and shooting, Patton ducked around the house to get out of the line of fire as bullets exploded on the adobe wall behind him.

Patton reloaded and popped out from behind the house just in time to see another rider bearing down on him. Resisting the urge to shoot the man, he instead lowered his pistol and shot the horse, which collapsed with the rider stuck in the saddle. The rider disentangled himself and was bringing his pistol around to fire when Patton and a few of his soldiers dispatched him. Patton, firing his rifle, and his men brought down a second man who was fleeing. The third Mexican was felled while running along a wall. He was the man whose arm was broken from Patton's opening volley. Although wounded with two bullet holes in his chest and one in his arm, the man offered to surrender, but when one of Patton's men approached him, he fired at the American, who shot him in the head, killing him.

The brief skirmish was over, but Patton was concerned that more bandits might be lurking in the ranch house and might fire on his men from the roof. With his men standing guard, Patton climbed a dead tree up to the roof. Upon stepping on the flimsy thatched structure, he fell through up to his armpits. He extricated himself and had his men search the house. They found only old men, women, and children. Through questioning they discovered one of the dead men was Villa's trusted commander Col. Julio Cardanes. Patton and his men strapped the dead Mexicans to the hoods of their cars and collected all the weapons and saddles they could. Before racing back to camp, Patton stopped his little caravan to cut the town's telephone wire so no other bandits could be alerted. Patton reported back to a pleased Pershing.[17]

Patton's Rubio Ranch action was the campaign's highpoint. With nothing to show for his efforts, Pershing withdrew his force to within 150 miles of the border. There he trained the men in mock battles, used competitive sports to keep them fit, and conducted wholesale inspections. One evening Patton was in his tent writing a paper when his gasoline lamp exploded and badly burned his face and head. The injuries turned out to be superficial, and after recuperating in a hospital, he received sick leave back at Fort Riley. He and Bea took the train to California, where he helped in his father's campaign for election to the U.S. Senate. Bandaged, in uniform, and well known for his adventures in Mexico, Patton sat onstage while his father made speeches. But it was for naught; his father lost the election.[18]

As the American forces departed Mexico in February 1917, Patton could be proud of his accomplishments. He had led a daring raid and remained cool and unafraid under fire. He had carried out the first motorized combat mission in U.S. Army history. He became aware of airpower, watching flimsy Army planes conduct reconnaissance over Mexico. He learned the importance of logistics and field communications. Most important, he served under Pershing, whom he modeled himself after. The way Pershing carried himself, issued orders, enforced discipline, and earned loyalty struck Patton deeply. These qualities would become Patton's in the decades to come.[19]

Soon Patton and Pershing were linked again. The United States declared war on Imperial Germany on April 6, 1917, and Pershing was selected to train a division and lead it overseas to fight on the side of Great Britain and France. He requested Patton to accompany him with a small contingent of troops as a symbol of reassurance to the war-weary Allies. On the trip across the Atlantic, Patton busied himself with improving his French. The War Department planned to send Pershing two million troops to be trained on their arrival in France.

Patton, now a captain, was in charge of 250 men who made up the Headquarters Company, as well as a motorcar detachment of ninety cars, which helped him continue his study of the combustion engine. His other duties included antiaircraft defense and enforcing discipline in dress and military comportment. His duties were not burdensome, and he had time for other exploits. In June Col. Billy Mitchell took Patton for his first flight in a biplane. "I had always though it would frighten me but it did not," he wrote in his diary. "The entire country spreads out like a map beneath you and it is fine."[20]

One duty Patton must have found distasteful was keeping his sister away from Europe and General Pershing. Nita and the general had become close before the Punitive Expedition and continued to see each other afterward. The newspapers caught a picture of the couple when she accompanied him to his ship for Europe and announced that they were engaged. Once in Europe, however, Pershing became busy with the war, and Patton continually wrote Beatrice explaining that it would be impossible for Nita to come over. Besides Pershing's schedule and the fact that having his girlfriend visit him from across the Atlantic while his men suffered in the trenches would be distasteful, there was another reason to keep Nita at a distance. Pershing had fallen in love with another woman in France. While Patton must certainly have known about his boss's dalliances—the two often dined together and discussed Nita—Patton never reported them to anyone in his family and helped protect Pershing's image.[21]

Pershing took Patton along when he visited the French and British commanders to plan the American troops' role in the fighting. Patton impressed Field Marshal Douglas Haig, the commander of the British Expeditionary Force, as "a fire-eater [who] longs for the fray."[22] But the fire-eater was getting bored with his job and wanted to leave his duties for the front. Opportunity came in the form of a new, barely tested weapon of war: the tank. Both the British and French had employed tanks, with the British using heavy models, the French light ones. The U.S. Army had neither, but there was much discussion among officers about fielding the new contraption.

Putting his name on a list of candidates for the potential tank unit, Patton sent a letter with his qualifications to the officers who were beginning the tank corps. He compared the deployment of light tanks to cavalry operations in offensive maneuvering. He said he was familiar with machine guns, as he had commanded a machine-gun troop. He knew automobile motors, for he had worked on them, and he was one of the few officers on Pershing's staff who actually owned a car in France. He was the only American to have made an attack in a motor vehicle. He was an experienced teacher. Finally, he spoke French.

Promoted to major, Patton was ordered to start a tank school in the town of Langres. He worried about the enterprise until he decided that, as the first tanker, he would be the only officer in light tanks in the American Expeditionary Force. He set off to learn everything he could. He spent a week at the French school near Compiègne and drove a Renault tank, fired its machine guns and cannons, observed maneuvers, studied the tank machinery and structure, inspected repair shops, and spoke with teachers and students about tank deployments. He spent another week at the tank factory in Paris.

At this point the British launched their first major tank attack of the war at Cambrai. The lumbering giants, almost five hundred in all, gained seven miles in four hours, something unheard of in trench warfare, where advances were usually measured in yards. Although the British lost most of the ground to a German counterattack—they could not sustain momentum in the new machines—the initial success had an electric effect on the U.S. Army. Scores of officers now wanted to be in the tank corps. Patton visited Cambrai shortly after the battle and talked with the British officers and men.

The reports Patton wrote about tanks became the foundation of U.S. operations with this new instrument of war. Leaving the considerable comfort of Pershing's headquarters for Langres, he vowed to do his best. His immediate boss, another member of Pershing's staff, was Col. Samuel D. Rochenbach, who looked after both the light tanks under Patton and heavy tank training in England.[23] "Now I rise and fall on my own," Patton wrote. Nervous about his role, he reassured himself by saying, "I could never look myself in the face if I was a staff officer and relatively safe."[24]

The town of Langres, about twenty miles from Pershing's headquarters in Chaumont, was crowded with American headquarters and units. Searching for terrain that could support his tanks in training, Patton found what he wanted at the hamlet of Bourg, five miles from Langres, on a main road and railway. After receiving the ground from the French authorities, he took Rochenbach on a tour of French and English tank schools and installations, explaining technical affairs and bringing the boss into his own outlook.

The first two hundred of Patton's future tankers arrived near the end of the year. He greeted them with a hot meal and he tried to make them comfortable, but he expected them to measure up to his standards. "The Tank Corps," he wrote, "will have discipline if nothing else." Lacking tanks, the men went through a training program to prepare them for combat. He stressed military courtesy, feeling that if an officer could not get his men to salute, he could not get them to follow orders in combat.[25]

Late in March, ten tanks arrived by train. Patton had already had a ramp built to take them off the railroad cars. Because he was the only one who knew anything about the new vehicles, he drove each one off himself. He showed nine men how to maneuver the tanks, then led them to a woods where they were put under camouflage. Having expected the task to take fifteen hours, he accomplished it in three.[26]

Patton pushed men and tanks to the limit of endurance. At the end of August 1918, Patton, now a lieutenant colonel, had enough men (nine hundred) and tanks (twenty-five) to organize the 1st Light Tank Brigade. Two months later, he changed the name to the 1st Tank Brigade. Even as he planned and supervised the training in Bourg, Patton attended the Army General Staff College in Langres. He also lectured on tank tactics, stressing the use of tanks to facilitate infantry attacks.[27]

No detail was too small for Patton. When he saw that infantry divisions were wearing distinctive shoulder patches, he held a contest to develop an insignia for tanks. A pair of lieutenants won by presenting him with a triangle made up of blue, yellow, and red, the colors for the infantry, cavalry, and artillery, respectively, since the tank corps was made up of elements of all three. Patton immediately gave the lieutenants $100 to go into town to have patches made for the whole brigade. The U.S. Army still uses the insignia today.[28]

In late August Patton had his chance to prove what he had been working for. He and his tanks were to be included in the St. Mihiel offensive, the first major action by American forces. Together with a French tank unit under his command, he would support the U.S. 1st and 42nd Infantry divisions. In great excitement, he reconnoitered the ground where he would launch his tanks, accompanying a patrol into no-man's-land.

The offensive began on September 12 with a four-hour artillery barrage. Frustrated because he could not see what was happening up front in the foggy morning, Patton left his command post and walked two miles onto the battlefield. He helped liberate a few tanks bogged down in mud. Once he saw that his tanks were moving, he decided not to return to his headquarters and remained at the front. He kept walking forward, passing through artillery fire and enemy trenches, all the while urging his men on. He joined Brig. Gen. Douglas MacArthur on a small hill just as an artillery barrage passed over. They talked with one another while others ducked for cover.

Noticing his tanks stopped at a bridge into the town of Essey, one of his objectives, Patton hurried there. The tankers were unwilling to cross the bridge because someone had told them that the Germans had mined it. As soon as the Americans tried to cross, they reasoned, the enemy would blow up the structure. Nonsense, Patton thought, and he walked across. Nothing happened. The tankers quickly followed him and took the village, where Germans surrendered to him and MacArthur.

Patton continued on to the next town, Pannes, but the drive was too much for his tanks; all but one had run out of gas. When the supporting infantry refused to go forward, Patton mounted the one operable tank and rode on it into the town, passing dead German bodies, mangled horses, and wrecked equipment along the way. Once in the town, the tankers, using only pistols, gathered up thirty German prisoners.

Suddenly, a concealed German machine gunner opened fire on the tank. Patton, noticing that the paint on the side of the tank was flying off, leaped from the tank and landed in a shallow shell hole. The tankers, not realizing their commander had departed, continued on, leaving Patton stranded. After figuring out a route for retreat and tiring of listening to the fire overhead, Patton began a sideways movement back to the infantry, dropping every time he heard the machine gun open fire. After failing to coax any of the infantry to retrieve his tank, Patton drew a deep breath and took off for it. "I was not scared," he confided to his diary, "I did however run like H——." Patton reached the tank amid fierce German fire. The tank driver saluted him, and Patton ordered him back until reinforcements arrived. He led the tank back, keeping it between himself and the German fire. Once back, four more tanks rolled up, and Patton had them take the next town, Beney. There was little firing from the town. "The tanks had scarred the Boche away."[29]

The battle continued another day, but the tankers had made a great contribution to its success. Patton's men proved the value of tanks in combat. Newspaper accounts raved about the daring tankers and their commander.[30]

There was no time to celebrate. The entire First U.S. Army was set to move to the Meuse-Argonne to launch another offensive. Patton's tanks would again be in support, this time operating with the I Corps. Once again, Patton conducted a personal reconnaissance of the battlefield. On September 26 the attack began after a three-hour artillery barrage. Again, Patton moved forward to motivate and coordinate his men.[31]

Near the hamlet of Cheppy, the enemy fire intensified. Patton and his small party took cover and saw their infantry beginning to withdraw. Patton stopped them. He gathered about one hundred men and led them to the base of the reverse slope of a hill. Discovering several tanks behind him and halted by an immense trench, he sent several men and eventually went himself to dig out the sides of the trenches. He refused to let the men duck from enemy artillery as they worked to break down the trench sides. After these exertions, five tanks were able to advance.[32]

Patton led the men up the hill, but as they reached the top, German fire forced them to dive to the ground. Patton was scared and trembling. He looked skyward and saw a strange thing. His ancestors were in a cloud, looking down at him. It was time, he decided, for another Patton to make the ultimate sacrifice. Becoming calm, he gathered up his men and said, "Let's go."[33]

The men followed but began falling from the enemy fire. Soon Patton was advancing with only his orderly, Joe Angelo, at his side. A German bullet struck Patton's left thigh and brought him down. Angelo pulled him into a shell hole and applied first aid. Although wounded, Patton sent Angelo over to several tanks to point out German positions. Hours later, when it was safe, a stretcher team arrived and removed Patton from the battlefield. He insisted on going to division headquarters so he could report on the situation before going to the hospital.

While recuperating, Patton was promoted to colonel. Later he received the Distinguished Service Cross for gallantry in combat and the Distinguished Service Medal for distinction in a post of high responsibility. He was at Bourg, working on a paper about tank tactics when the war ended on his birthday, November 11, 1918.[34]

His service in Mexico and particularly in France had proved his leadership as well as his methods. His men had been proficient and aggressive in battle. He himself had made a difference in every fight. He was indeed a first-rate soldier. But had he then fulfilled his destiny, his fate?

The Long Wait

T he war's end brought an end to the excitement and glory. Apathy set in during the interwar period. Rapid demobilization, congressional penny-pinching, and the rise of pacifism together with national isolationism downsized the Army and made it stagnant. Patton approached middle-age and began to wonder whether his dreams of fame would go unfulfilled.

In the war's immediate aftermath, Patton maintained discipline of his men, read about and experimented with tanks, and pondered the concept of marrying tanks with the role of the cavalry, an idea that would be known in World War II as "blitzkrieg." Meanwhile, he watched from afar as his sister arrived in London to meet with Pershing and the two decided to end their relationship. In 1919 Patton led his men onto a troopship for the journey home. On arriving in New York, he stole away to Mitchell Field for a reunion with Bea while his men headed to Fort Meade, Maryland. There they joined with tankers training at Camp Colt, Pennsylvania, near Gettysburg, under Lt. Col. Dwight D. Eisenhower.[1]

At Meade, Patton trained his tankers with Eisenhower, wrote a tank manual, improved tank equipment, and helped designer J. Walter

Christie develop a new and revolutionary tank chassis that could run on both treads and wheels. While Patton's relationship with the brilliant but eccentric Christie was professional, he found a true friend in Eisenhower. When not drilling troops, the two had long talks about tank tactics and other military matters while their wives visited. The two officers would even go for late-night drives, packing pistols and looking for trouble. Eisenhower hoped he would serve under Patton during the next big war.[2]

The National Defense Act of June 1920 slashed military spending, abolished the tanks' independent role, and placed the tank corps in the infantry branch.[3] Unwilling to serve in the no-longer-autonomous tanks corps, Patton returned to the cavalry and to his permanent rank of captain. The day after he rejoined the cavalry, he was promoted to major and stationed at Fort Myer as a squadron commander. He played polo, participated in horse shows, took part in races, and rode to the hounds. He coined several aphorisms in his lectures and writings: A general should not live to explain his defeat. An imperfect solution applied at once is worth more than a perfect solution later. Success in war depends on speed, simplicity, and boldness. A commander is never defeated until he admits it. The fog of war covers the enemy too.[4]

Beatrice gave birth to a boy in December 1920, and they named him George Smith IV. Patton had begun attending the Command and General Staff College at Fort Leavenworth, Kansas, and there he flourished. Shortly after his son was born, he graduated in the top 25 percent of his class, but he was almost kicked out of the school at the outset. When another student spied him studying one night under a blue light, an academic board ordered him to explain himself. An embarrassed Patton explained that the blue light was not a forbidden study aid but a light bulb that was supposed to restore his hair.[5]

As a general staff corps officer, Patton was assigned to Boston as G-1, director of personnel. After eight months, he was transferred to Schofield Barracks and the Hawaiian Division as G-1 and G-2, director of intelligence. He enjoyed the climate, the social life, and the polo at Schofield. Soon after he was appointed G-3, director of plans and training, he was relieved because of his abrasive nature, his impatience with mistakes, and his denunciation of errors committed by superior officers.[6]

Patton's parents died while he was in Hawaii. He transferred his share of their estate to his sister Nita. Three years later, Aunt Nannie passed away. Patton tortured himself with the thought that he had been unable to win the fame they had expected of him while they were alive.[7]

Judged by his superior officers as "invaluable in war . . . but a disturbing element in times of peace," Patton felt complimented.[8] Transferred in 1928 to the Office of the Chief of Cavalry in Washington, D.C., he became involved in the debates over mechanization in the Army. At that time, tanks were considered important for wars fought in areas where road nets existed, whereas horses were desired where roads were nonexistent. Experiments with mechanized warfare were limited, however, because of frugal military budgets. At Patton's urging, the cavalry tested a few armored cars.

While explaining the classic fire and maneuver tactic, Patton coined an unforgettable phrase. Referring to pinning down the enemy with fire and attacking him in the flank or rear, Patton said, "Grab him by the nose and kick him in the pants."[9]

Patton attended the Army War College in 1931. His paper on how the Army should prepare for the next war was so well received that the college sent it to the War Department General Staff for consideration. Returning to Fort Myer shortly thereafter, Patton became the executive officer of a cavalry regiment.[10]

In 1932, at the height of the Great Depression, approximately twenty thousand veterans from around the country flocked to Washington, D.C., to demand an immediate payment of a bonus voted for disbursement in 1945. The Bonus Marchers lived in dismantled or partially built houses inside the U.S. Capitol grounds and in a makeshift camp across the Anacostia River. They were orderly, if restless, but their numbers worried the president, his secretary of war, and the U.S. Army chief of staff, General MacArthur. When Congress adjourned for the summer without voting to advance the bonus, some of the veterans left the city but others stayed.

On July 28 President Herbert Hoover ordered the Army to remove the Bonus Marchers. Troops of the 3rd Cavalry left Fort Myer and headed to the ellipse behind the White House to join with the 16th Infantry coming in from Fort Washington downriver. Patton, who was not required to be there, reconnoitered ahead, meeting both cheers and jeers from the veterans. Late that afternoon the cavalry started down Pennsylvania Avenue, with the infantry following. As they proceeded, violence broke out. Marchers started throwing rocks and bricks while the cavalrymen whacked the marchers with the flats of their swords and infantrymen prodded them with their bayonets. Once order was restored, MacArthur directed the troops to march across the Anacostia River and eject the veterans from their camp. Some tents and huts started to burn and soon the entire camp was consumed in flames. The Bonus Marchers departed the city.

Patton was involved in an embarrassing incident the day after the eviction. He and a few other soldiers were manning a picket line when a small band of marchers approached. With them was Joe Angelo, who had bandaged Patton's wound in the shell hole in France. Patton denied knowing Angelo and ordered him taken away. After the war, Angelo, who could not find work, had written Patton asking for help and Patton would often send him money. When Angelo had come to Washington a year before the march to speak to a committee about the veterans' plight, Beatrice took her children to meet him and hear the tale the children had heard so many times from their father. But the Bonus March changed the relationship between the two men. Patton and Angelo were on different sides of a potential riot. Patton worried what the press would say about an officer who turned his back on the former orderly who saved his life. But duty came first. He cut his ties with Angelo, although he did send him money in 1939, when he heard that the old veteran was still in need.[11]

As a result of the Bonus March, Patton wrote a number of papers on suppressing riots and insurrections that were quite brutal. They suggested employing snipers to eliminate a riot's leaders, using gas, and killing resisters. Reversing Napoleon's logic of killing only a few rebels when putting down a riot, Patton encouraged killing many: "a few casualties become martyrs, a large number is an object lesson."[12]

Promoted to lieutenant colonel and assigned again to Hawaii, Patton sailed to Honolulu on his yacht, the *Arcturus,* in May 1935. Acting as captain and navigator, he launched from Catalina, California, with a small crew, including Beatrice. A trip across the Pacific was no small task, but they made it, even though Beatrice, a lifelong boater, spent most of the journey seasick. The yacht arrived in Honolulu to a huge welcoming party. A band played, girls in hula skirts danced, and family and friends cheered the weary travelers.[13]

Assigned as G-2, director of intelligence, for the Hawaiian Department at Fort Shafter, Patton wrote a plan to "maintain internal security and censorship" on the islands in the event of war with Japan. The outline was brutal and called for arresting and interning Japanese residents and holding them as hostages rather than as prisoners. These recommendations reflected the recent Japanese conquest of Manchuria and the vulnerability of Hawaii to Japanese air and sea attack.[14]

Patton soon became bored with his duties as G-2. He was concerned that the position was a dead-end job. Despairing over his prospects, he began drinking too much. His frustrations also showed on the polo fields. During an interisland championship game, he cursed the opposing team's captain when his horse collided with the horse of his good friend Walter Dillingham. Patton shouted, "Goddammit, Walter, you old son of a bitch," in his high-pitched voice. The commanding general overheard the remark and ejected Patton from the match. But his opponents said they had not heard his swear and refused to play without him. The general rescinded the order, and the match continued. In another game, Patton suffered a concussion that caused surprising mood swings whenever he drank even a small amount of spirits. It would forever affect him.[15]

Patton's despair over his career led him into an extramarital affair. Jean Gordon, Patton's niece on Beatrice's side of the family, visited Hawaii on her way to the Orient. She adored Patton, and the timing of her trip could not have been worse. Beatrice had spent the second tour of Hawaii toiling on a novel that she would entitle *The Blood of the Shark*, a romance about a ship captain and the daughter of a Hawaiian chieftain in 1793. Patton was unsupportive and even resented Bea for the attention she received for her efforts. Jean showered Patton with affection when she arrived on the island, and soon the twenty-one-year-old girl—who was the same age as Patton's daughter Ruth Ellen—and the forty-two-year-old lieutenant colonel began an affair that lasted the duration of Jean's visit. When she left the islands, Patton waved frantically from the end of the pier. Beatrice considered leaving him over his infidelity, but decided against it, telling Ruth Ellen, "I am all that he really has."[16]

When his Hawaiian tour ended in 1937, Patton sailed his yacht back across the Pacific, this time with his young son added to the crew. The family returned to Massachusetts, as the world seemed to disintegrate into war—the Japanese had invaded China, Adolf Hitler's Germany was rearming and threatening war, the Italians were engaged in Africa, and Spain had begun a civil war. One day Patton went for a horseback ride with Bea. In the midst of the outing, Bea's horse bolted and kicked Patton, fracturing his leg in two places. He spent six months on his back, during which time a blood clot almost took his life. When he could walk, it was with an iron brace. He limped, and the leg swelled after use.[17]

Fortunately, a medical exam showed Patton capable of limited service. He was assigned to Fort Riley to teach at the Cavalry School. While there, he exercised until he brought himself back to his former health. He also became acquainted with a man who would accompany him wherever he went for the rest of his days. Pvt. George Meeks lived with the Patton's cook, Vergie, who was married—though not to Meeks. The Pattons corrected the situation, and soon, the quiet soldier began ironing Patton's clothes, shining his boots, and taking care of the lieutenant colonel's needs. Meeks, who had served in Russia after World War I fighting the Bolsheviks, could neither read nor write and had remained a private despite more than fifteen years in the Army. His association with Patton would eventually bring him the rank of sergeant first class.[18]

As war clouds continued to gather around the world, Patton was next sent to Fort Clark, Texas, to command a regiment of the 1st Cavalry Division. His new assignment pleased him, for he was commanding troops again and preparing for war.

A telephone call from Washington, D.C., spoiled his endeavors, however. He was ordered to take command of Fort Myer because Jonathan Wainwright was unable to afford the expenses of heading this showpiece post. Patton felt sick at heart to give up his exciting command in the field, but his luck changed in the spring of 1939, when George C. Marshall became acting chief of staff of the U.S. Army. While

Marshall's house at Fort Myer was being repaired and refurbished, he moved in temporarily with his old friend Patton. Patton's performance during spring maneuvers proved to Marshall the lieutenant colonel's unflagging energy and professionalism.[19]

On the outbreak of war in Europe on September 1, 1939, Patton began to reevaluate his idea of using tanks as cavalry. The German blitzkrieg in Poland demonstrated a new concept of their employment. Patton studied reports of the German campaign avidly. His assignment as an umpire in the Texas maneuvers of 1940 brought him up to date on American tank equipment and theory.[20]

The German defeat of Poland, but especially the more disturbing German victories in the Low Countries and France in the spring of 1940, prompted Marshall to establish the Armored Force, with its mission to develop tank warfare to match and overcome the Germans. Patton received command of a brigade of the 2nd Armored Division at Fort Benning.[21]

Back again with the tanks and preparing seriously for war, Patton was overjoyed. Perhaps his dreams of fame and glory were still reachable. With a bit of luck he might find the Holy Grail. To Patton, the wonderful thing about this assignment to the Armored Force was the motivation it provided. He was again with the troops who needed discipline, proficiency, and aggressiveness, all Patton trademarks, as they prepared for battle. He drove them, cajoled them, and quickly trained them in his likeness, all the while studying how to use the new instruments and formations of modern war.

He also became well known to the public. He advertised his men, provided good copy for newspaper reporters, and before long made the public aware of how powerful his tanks were. In December 1940, with much advance publicity, he took his unit on a march from Columbus, Georgia, to Panama City, Florida, a distance of four hundred miles, to test and practice procedures and discipline but also to capture public attention not only for himself but also for the Armored Force. Thousands of spectators, including children excused from school, watched in wonder at the seemingly endless procession of vehicles—tanks, trucks, and Jeeps—roaring along the roads. The action was well covered in the newspapers, causing a spark among World War I veterans who had served with Patton. Many tried to reenlist but were too old to fight. One exception was Alexander Stiller, a former sergeant who attended officer candidate school and joined Patton's staff. Also joining Patton was Richard N. Jensen, the son of family friends in California.[22]

In April 1941 Patton received his second star as the commanding general of the 2nd Armored Division. He participated in the Tennessee Maneuvers in June, a series of large-scale sham battles to test the proficiency of units and commanders. His division was spectacular and unorthodox, and its aggressive action brought problems to a quick resolution, in one case completing a two-day exercise in nine hours.

In August and September Patton and his division took part in war games taking place in Louisiana and Texas. Again, the 2nd Armored Division and its commander were stars by virtue of their daring and proficiency. Patton superbly managed control and coordination. They repeated their performance in the Carolina Maneuvers in November.[23]

Shortly after the Japanese attack on Pearl Harbor, Patton was placed in command of the I Armored Corps. He now controlled and directed the 1st and 2nd Armored divisions. In February 1942 he was ordered to create and to operate a desert training area, which would duplicate the conditions of fighting in Libya and Egypt, where the Germans and Italians were struggling with the British.[24]

Flying to Riverside, California, in March 1942, Patton reconnoitered from the air a vast wasteland including parts of California, Nevada, and Arizona. With incredible speed he organized a training center and opened it in April. The only way to start things, he said, "is to start." He put units though a series of exhausting field exercises. The only shelter were tents without electricity, lights, heat, or hot water. Cots lacked sheets, and men were limited to one canteen of water a day. They would run a mile in ten minutes, march eight miles in two hours every day, and go without sleep periodically.[25] The regimen not only hardened the men but also demonstrated the deprivations of warfare. Patton was everywhere, inspecting, cursing, complimenting, and finding fault as well as successes in equipment, weapons, and procedures. He kept both Jacob Devers, head of the Armored Force, and Leslie J. McNair, in charge of training combat troops, informed of his findings.[26]

Marshall soon sent Eisenhower and Mark W. Clark to England to establish the European Theater of Operations, U.S. Army, and he called Patton to Washington, D.C., in June 1942.[27] When Prime Minister Winston Churchill was meeting with President Franklin Roosevelt, news arrived that Field Marshal Erwin Rommel had captured Tobruk, Libya, a British strong point. Marshall offered to send an American armored division to Egypt to help the British. He asked Patton to plan the reinforcement. After studying the situation, Patton recommended sending two armored divisions. By this time, Marshall had changed his mind as the plan would take too long to accomplish. Instead, he furnished the British three hundred tanks and one hundred howitzers.[28]

No longer needed, Patton returned to his Desert Training Center. Uninformed on Marshall's decision, he was sure that he had committed a grave error by recommending two divisions instead of the one originally offered. Hoping that he had not antagonized the chief of staff, Patton let it be known that henceforth he would take anything and go anyplace anytime without asking any questions.[29]

Two months later, when the president decided to invade French North Africa with American and British troops, Patton was named to lead American soldiers sailing directly from the United States to the beaches of Morocco. Patton quickly summarized his observation of what the Desert Training Center had proved, then traveled to Washington at the end of July. He became acquainted with the operation, code-named Torch, and, on August 5, flew to London to confer with Eisenhower, the Allied commander.[30] Patton spent three weeks in London devising a plan with Eisenhower and Clark, the deputy commander and chief planner. The expedition seemed extremely risky so Patton promised to "succeed or die trying."[31]

Eventually, the plan consisted of three landings: Patton's on the Atlantic coast of French Morocco and two American and British invasions on the Mediterranean coast of Algeria. The invasions would introduce the inexperienced Americans to war against the armed forces of Vichy France. The landings would also threaten Rommel's Italo-German army. The fighting was hoped to take some pressure off the Russians, who seemed close to defeat. Allied possession of North Africa would also provide territory from which to launch future offensives.[32]

Patton and his twenty-four thousand troops battle loaded and sailed in one hundred ships from Norfolk, Virginia. Patton used the time to read the Koran, exercise in his cabin, and write in his diary. The landings were scheduled for November 8. Early that day, the high winds of the Moroccan shore stilled and the sea calmed. As Patton prepared to go ashore, the French reacted with sporadic gunfire. The same thing occurred in Oran and Algiers. Yet the soldiers in all three landings managed to get ashore and seize their objectives.[33]

North Africa and Sicily

P atton's men made three separate landings in Morocco: at Safi, about 150 miles southwest of Casablanca; at Fedala, fifteen miles north of Casablanca; and at Mahdia, fifty miles north of Casablanca. Patton had planned to go ashore with the main landing at Fedala, until seven French cruisers burst from a smoke screen and began firing on the American fleet. The Americans replied, and the muzzle blasts from Patton's ship blew his awaiting landing craft to splinters. Oddly enough, just moments before he had ordered Sergeant Meeks to retrieve his ivory-handled pistols from the landing craft before it was destroyed. Patton stayed on board and watched the action, getting wet from geysers erupting around the ship.[1]

He finally stepped ashore that afternoon, soaking wet and in a bad mood. What he saw on the beach did not encourage him. Men who were supposed to be setting up signal corps stations, medical tents, and supply depots were, instead, digging foxholes for protection from sporadic shell fire. Patton went into action, organizing men, shouting at them, kicking them in the pants, and cajoling them into doing their jobs. He restored order and purpose. He returned the next day at dawn, like the wrath of God, galvanizing men into action. By noon, landing operations were running smoothly and supplies were being distributed on shore.[2]

Patton's green troops were struggling against the Vichy French, but they were making steady progress. His men met the stiffest resistance on the northern-most landing beach, at Mahdia. There, elements of the 3rd Infantry Division were held up at a castle called the Kasbah. Patton was too far south of the castle to make a difference with his presence, but he followed the fight closely. When his troops finally stormed the Kasbah and ended resistance, Patton described his men fighting "with bayonets and hand grenades in true movie style."[3]

Patton returned to his ship and had the supply ships move closer to shore to speed the off-loading of supplies. He then began planning the attack on Casablanca. He wanted his green troops to attack at 7:30 a.m. to ensure they would not become confused in the darkness. Although he regretted it later, he also planned to have the city bombed and shelled. With his plan set, he went to sleep, only to be awakened by an intelligence officer at 4:30 a.m. on November 11. The French were preparing to surrender, should the attack be called off? No, Patton said, not until they had actually capitulated. Less than an hour before the attack was set to take place, the French surrendered. Patton considered this "a nice birthday present." He was fifty-seven years old.[4]

That afternoon, the French commanders were escorted into Patton's headquarters in the Hotel Miramar in Fedala. After complimenting the French on their gallantry, he had an officer read two approved versions of an armistice agreement. The first, assuming token French resistance, offered lenient treatment. The second, supposing protracted fighting until total French defeat, dictated harsher terms, including the disarming and disbanding of the French army.[5] Neither treaty applied to the situation at hand. Unwilling to become involved in local security problems, Patton struck a compromise and proposed a gentleman's agreement. The Americans could have access to whatever they needed to fight the Axis, prisoners would be exchanged, and the French troops, with their arms intact, would be confined to their barracks for the time being. The French agreed. With the negotiations over, Patton startled his French visitors. One more "disagreeable formality needed settling," he said. He produced champagne for all and toasted the end of fighting as well as the return to the old alliance between France and America.[6]

Patton's success confirmed his genius. He showed flair in his military as well as diplomatic efforts. He impressed all, not only those in the theater but those at home, who began to take note of his qualities and personality. He realized it too. He took numerous photographs of himself on the battlefield and at the sites of his attacks and successes. One picture in particular, of himself on the Fedala beach, so impressed Patton that he sent it home and suggested to his wife it might make a good magazine cover.[7]

Meanwhile, the invasion of Algiers and Oran had succeeded. Maj. Gen. Mark Clark had hurried from Eisenhower's headquarters in Gibraltar to Algiers to meet with Adm. Jean Darlan, an important figure in the Vichy administration as well as commander of Vichy's armed forces, who happened to have been visiting his son, who was in the hospital with polio. Clark hammered out the Darlan deal that brought the French in North Africa into the Allied camp. The war moved eastward to Tunisia, but Patton remained in Morocco with little to do.[8]

Patton became sick at heart when he learned of Clark's promotion to lieutenant general and his subsequent command of the newly formed U.S. Fifth Army headquarters. Henry T. Stimson, the secretary of war, had intimated that Patton would receive those rewards, but it was not to be. Nevertheless, Patton sent Clark a letter of congratulations.[9]

Patton made Casablanca a first-class base, improving its airfields and increasing its logistical capacity. He whipped new recruits into shape. Mainly, he worked to keep the relations between the Americans and French amicable. And he was careful not to neglect the native rulers. He kept the country calm and the French cooperative. He spent much time attending ceremonies by the French and the sultan of Morocco.

For leisure, Patton accompanied the sultan on hunting and fishing expeditions. These were elaborate productions employing hundreds of servants. During the hunts, the servants flushed animals out into the open for Patton or the sultan to shoot. For fishing, the servants set up tent cities near well-established fishing spots. Patton's only real connection with the war was the occasional night bombings that came from the German Luftwaffe.[10]

Bored with his job in Casablanca, Patton visited the war front, officially to report on the failures of American armor but really to be near the fighting. During his visit he came across his son-in-law, Lt. Col. John Waters, a battalion commander with the 1st Armored Division. Stopping to chat in the middle of the desert, Patton noticed that Waters looked tired and that he had a bullet hole in his coat. Patton was proud that his son-in-law was a fighter.[11]

The troops at the front appreciated Patton's presence, telling him he was the only general they had seen at the front in more than three weeks. A sad commentary, Patton thought. The Allies were fighting an inefficient war against a well-organized and battle-hardened enemy. He saw drunken generals, an ineffective supply system, poor tactical procedures, and a lack of unity among the Allied forces.[12]

He laid the blame on Eisenhower and Clark and their poor leadership, calling them "glamour boys" who were "too damned slick" with no idea what was happening at the front. Eisenhower was too pro-British for Patton. "Ike is not commanding," Patton confided in his diary, and he was allowing political and economic problems to divert his attention from the war front. Patton kept his complaints to himself, though, for he realized that he needed Eisenhower's good graces if he was to see any fighting.[13]

Early in January 1943, the Fifth Army was activated and Patton's I Armored Corps and Lloyd Fredendall's II Corps came under Clark. Fredendall moved into southern Tunisia as part of British general Kenneth Anderson's First Army. The front was static, but Field Marshal Rommel's Italo-German army was approaching Tunisia, retreating out of Libya, and was pursued by British general Sir Bernard L. Montgomery, after his victory at El Alamein.[14]

In mid-January 1943, Patton was put in charge of hosting the Casablanca Conference, where President Roosevelt and Prime Minister Churchill, together with their military advisers, met to determine the direction of the war. Patton made arrangements for all the guests and provided security. While he did not partake in the meetings where strategy was discussed, he met with all the principals and dined with most of them. Whenever he was complimented on his troops' appearance and his hospitality, he responded with his hope for a command in combat.[15]

Cadet Patton at West Point in 1909. (Patton Museum)

Patton training for the 1912 Olympic Games in Stockholm. (Patton Museum)

First Lieutenant Patton in Mexico, on the Punitive Expedition, 1916. (National Archives)

Colonel Patton (third from the left) with Maj. Gen. Henry T. Allen in France after World War I. (National Archives)

Lieutenant Colonel Patton in front of a Renault tank in Bourg, France, 1918.
(National Archives)

Patton and Beatrice with daughters Ruth Ellen and Little Bea. (Patton Museum)

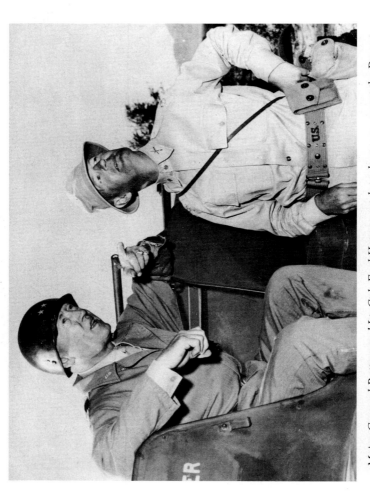

Major General Patton and Lt. Col. Earl Horan watch tanks maneuver at the Desert Training Center in California. (National Archives)

Patton prepares to head to shore off Morocco during Operation Torch.
(National Archives)

Lieutenant General Patton, II Corps commander, watches his tanks advance on the Tunisian front. (National Archives)

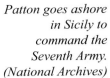

Patton goes ashore in Sicily to command the Seventh Army. (National Archives)

Patton puffs a cigar on the streets of Gela, Sicily.
(National Archives)

*Patton delivers a speech to a woman's club in Knutsford, England.
The speech got him in trouble. (National Archives)*

Gen. Dwight D. Eisenhower, Patton, Lt. Gen. Omar Bradley, and Lt. Gen. Courtney Hodges hold an impromptu meeting in the field. (National Archives)

Patton packs a pistol into his holster during the breakout in France. (National Archives)

Patton wraps up against the cold during the winter battles along the German border. (National Archives)

Patton and Marshal Gregory Zhukov watch a victory parade in Berlin after the war. (National Archives)

Patton greets Beatrice after war. (National Archives)

*Patton receives the order of the White Lion and Military Cross
First Class from President Edvard Benes of Czechoslovakia.*

Pallbearers carry Patton's body through the train station at Luxembourg City on the way to the U.S. cemetery at Hamm. (National Archives)

Two of the decisions reached at the meeting put Patton on a roller coaster of emotion. First, Sir Harold Alexander was picked to be the Allied ground forces commander in Tunisia and the American II Corps was placed under British Army command. Second, the Allies planned to invade Sicily after victory in North Africa, and Patton was to command the American forces. Patton was ecstatic.[16]

But the war in North Africa was hardly over. On January 30 German forces in Tunisia attacked Faïd and then launched a crushing blow on February 14, driving American and French forces fifty miles westward, buffeting the Allies at the Sbiba and Kasserine passes, and inflicting a devastating defeat. Rommel, on the verge of a strategic victory that would have driven the Allies out of Tunisia, withdrew to await Montgomery's arrival in the east. The Battle of Kasserine Pass showed how inexperienced the American soldiers were. Furthermore, Fredendall lost control of his corps, which suffered more than 3,000 killed and wounded, 3,700 captured, and about 200 tanks destroyed.[17]

The American soldiers seemed unmotivated, and subsequently, training schedules back at home were revised to lengthen the learning process. The British wondered if their American ally had the strength and gumption to fight the Germans on a modern battlefield. Patton was sure that his own talents were being overlooked and wasted.[18]

In a sudden, surprising reversal, Eisenhower summoned Patton to Algiers on March 4. Meeting Patton at the airfield, Eisenhower gave him command of II Corps. Patton was to restore American prestige and self-respect and fire any ineffective leaders. Resolving to make good, Patton flew immediately to Constantine, where he was briefed on his mission. He was to draw the Germans away from Montgomery's attack —to threaten only, not attack.[19]

At II Corps headquarters, where Patton formally relieved Fredendall, he was appalled by the poor discipline. He immediately ordered improved dress and saluting. When he entered the mess tent at 7:00 a.m. on the morning after his arrival he found only one of his staff at breakfast. He ordered the mess to be closed in a half hour. That same day, he appointed Omar Bradley as his deputy commander. Bradley had been sent to II Corps to serve as Eisenhower's eyes and ears, but Patton was uncomfortable with Bradley in that role, hence he made the appointment.[20]

For the next week, Patton traveled throughout II Corps, flanked by motorcycle outriders and armored cars. With sirens screaming and foghorns blasting, he visited every battalion headquarters to instill the men with "an adequate hatred of the Germans." He insisted his men wear neckties, leggings, and helmets. He fined anyone for infractions of military courtesy, and he exhorted his troops to be aggressive and offensive-minded and to kill the enemy instead of dying for their country. He also provided better conditions, the best equipment and the warmest clothing, better mail deliveries, better food, and additional shower facilities.[21]

With his new command came his third star. "When I was a little boy," he wrote in his diary, "I did not know there were full generals. Now I want, and will get, four stars." He appreciated his new status, immediately posing for a photo with his rank on his overseas cap. He even adorned a tank with red metal plates with three stars on them and posed in front of it wearing a football helmet with his new rank on it.[22]

During the night of March 16, Patton's 1st Infantry Division advanced forty-five miles in a pouring rain and captured the town of Gafsa. The next morning, the division advanced ten miles and took El-Guettar.[23] Two panzer divisions tried to take back the village, but the Americans fought well. The Germans withdrew, leaving about thirty smoldering tanks. The Germans counterattacked again, but the Americans held their ground. El-Guettar was an important battle for the Americans as it signaled a complete turnaround from the panic manifested during the fighting at Kasserine. It was Patton's victory. He had had eleven days to prepare for combat, and his methods had worked. He visited the front lines when he could, despite his dread of incoming shells, land mines, and bombs. "I still get scarred [sic]," he confessed to his diary. "I think I'll never get used to it."[24]

The 1st Armored Division had less luck. Mud prevented the tanks from maneuvering. Patton wanted its commander, Maj. Gen. Orlando Ward, to attack, fearing that a stationary armored division invited an attack from Rommel. But the 1st Armored was going nowhere. Ward was dispirited and had not fully recovered from the shock of Kasserine. Patton ordered him to capture the Maknassy Heights. When Ward captured the town but not the heights, Patton regretted not leading the attack himself. Ward went for the heights but was repulsed, and Patton ordered him to personally lead the next assault. He did and took the heights temporarily until the Germans counterattacked. Eventually Patton relieved Ward. Patton needed aggressive commanders who would push forward without being asked.[25]

Patton pushed his corps eastward to jab the Axis flank. He put together a tank task force under C. C. Benson, one of his World War I tankers, but he was disappointed with its lack of progress. Hoping for a great victory, Patton hounded Benson. When Benson's leading units stopped before a minefield, Patton grew furious. With only a Jeep and a scout car ahead of him, Patton drove through the field with Benson's men following. Patton turned around after a few miles, knowing his behavior to be reckless. Shortly thereafter, Benson's men came into contact with British troops, but Patton's efforts to cut off the Germans had failed.[26]

During Benson's attack, Patton lost his young aide, Richard Jensen, who was killed when twelve German planes bombed Benson's headquarters. Patton blamed the Allied air forces for his aide's death in a written report. A war of words began with Alexander's air officer claiming II Corps to be unbattleworthy and charging Patton with using the air force as an alibi for failure on the ground. An enraged Patton demanded a public apology. Three air force generals visited Patton at his headquarters to discuss the situation. While they were talking, four German aircraft flew over, firing machine guns and dropping bombs. Part of the ceiling collapsed, though no one in the room was hurt. When someone asked Patton how he managed to stage the German raid, he said, "I'll be damned if I know, but if I could find the sons of bitches who flew those planes, I'd mail each one of them a medal." Air support for Patton's ground forces subsequently improved.[27]

As the Germans in Tunisia retreated and the Allies prepared for the final battle, Patton learned that the II Corps was to be pinched out of the front. He was furious and protested to Eisenhower and Alexander that the Americans must be allowed to fight in the name of national prestige. Patton won the argument, and the II Corps remained on the line.[28]

Patton seemed to be everywhere on the battlefield. He was shelled daily during his drives to the front. He visited hospitals, although he found them "pretty gruesome." He also visited command posts under fire. When one of his infantry regiments failed to take a ridge five times and had heavy casualties, Patton had the "personal idea" to shell it with twenty-five rounds of white phosphorous and twenty-five rounds of high explosives. The ridge was then taken without a loss.[29]

With II Corps assured a place in the final actions of North Africa, Patton turned control of the corps over to Bradley and returned to preparing for the invasion of Sicily. Patton had made a difference in Tunisia. In eleven days, he had made a demoralized corps ready for the offensive. He had instilled pride and a fighting spirit in the American soldier. Perhaps the greatest compliment paid him came from General Marshall, who wrote to Patton, "You have done a fine job and have justified our confidence in you." The Tunisia campaign ended in May as the British and French entered Tunis and the Americans captured Bizerte.[30]

Sicily was next. The initial plan was simple. Montgomery would land in the south at Syracuse while Patton's Seventh Army landed in the north at Palermo. With two ports seized, the two Allied forces would drive to Messina in the island's northeastern corner. But Montgomery disliked the plan, preferring to have the Americans land west of him, in a supporting role, while he drove to Messina. Eisenhower and the other senior commanders were busy in Tunisia and were unable to concentrate on alternative plans. In the end, they did not weigh in on the matter until Montgomery had his way. Patton would invade in the south, without a major port for supply.[31]

While Patton was displeased with his role, he was happy to have Bradley's II Corps under him. Patton's divisions consisted of Terry Allen's 1st Infantry Division, which had done so well at El-Guettar; Lucian Truscott's 3rd Infantry Division, which had landed with him in Morocco; Troy Middleton's untested 45th Infantry Division, coming directly from the United States; and Matthew Ridgway's green but highly trained 82nd Airborne Division. U.S. Army Rangers, who had proved their value all across the western desert, would also spearhead the amphibious attack.[32]

When Patton boarded the *Monrovia,* the flagship of the assault force, he commanded ninety thousand men for the initial attack. He addressed the men, complimenting them on "having been selected" for the invasion and for the "privilege to attack and destroy" the enemy. As for himself, he confided to his diary that he was suffering from the "shortness of breath I always have before a polo game."[33]

In the early morning darkness of July 10, more than seven Allied divisions, supported by naval artillery fires, began landing on the Sicilian shoreline. The British took Syracuse but were stopped at Augusta. The Americans, fighting high winds along their beaches, made it ashore at Gela. The previous night, paratroopers from the 82nd Airborne Division had landed inland to disrupt any German counterattacks. Unfortunately the paratroopers had been scattered, though they had fought well in small groups. When Patton landed the next day, he stopped in the town to visit the Rangers. Just then an Italian infantry division and a German panzer division attacked.[34]

The town exploded with combat. Patton ordered naval artillery fire, helped place mortars, and helped stiffen resistance. The sight of a three-star general running around the perimeter, placing mortars, and urging the men on had an electrifying effect. The attack was repulsed. Patton had encouraged the men to "kill every one of the goddamn bastards." By afternoon, with sixteen enemy tanks destroyed, Gela was solidly in American hands. He visited command posts and returned to the beach, where he stood unharmed during an enemy air bombardment, showing himself to his men. When he boarded his ship, the *Monrovia*, again that evening he felt he had earned his pay.[35]

That night Patton's initial success would be forgotten as a friendly fire disaster lit up the skies above Sicily. Patton realized he needed to reinforce his paratroopers and agreed to a risky night drop into his lines. He warned all his Army and Navy commanders about the drop, alerting them to the time and direction of the air fleet's arrival. Unfortunately, the Luftwaffe had bombed and strafed the beachhead that day, putting most of his troops on edge. Patton realized this and tried to call off the airdrop, but he was too late. To make matters worse, the planes flew in on a different course than assigned, confusing the men on the ground. As the last Luftwaffe planes left the area, the paratrooper-packed transports arrived over Gela. The men on the ground opened fire and soon the Navy joined in.

When it was all over, 23 planes had been shot down and 82 paratroopers had been killed, with 131 wounded and 16 missing. Paratroopers had been fired on as they landed. Others bailed out over the sea, some washing up on the shore days later. Upon learning about the disaster, Eisenhower fired off a note to Patton, calling the whole incident inexcusable and demanding Patton launch an investigation and severely punish whoever was responsible. Patton, taking it personally, was furious at the reprimand. He had done everything possible to avert disaster, but it was not enough. He accepted blame for the incident—"If they want a goat, I am it." His investigation found several factors responsible for the tragedy, all related to the fog of war. Enemy planes caused the troop carriers to change their courses, not everyone received word of the airdrop, and air and ground recognition signals were not the same. No one was punished for the incident, and it was covered up to keep it from the public.[36]

The friendly fire incident over, Patton focused on the advance. He pushed his men forward and was, again, constantly at the front. When told that the Germans were booby-trapping their dead, it did not bother him. He said in response that his men were killing the enemy instead of letting them surrender. He referred to dead enemy soldiers as "good Germans" and "good Huns."[37]

East of the Seventh Army, a frustrated Montgomery took control of a road separating the two armies that belonged to Bradley's II Corps. Montgomery did not tell his American colleagues or his superiors about his move until it was done. With the road in Montgomery's hands Patton had no chance of making it to Messina first.[38]

Alexander informed Patton about Montgomery's action and approved it because he still harbored doubts about American competence. The Seventh Army's new job, Alexander reiterated, was to protect the British left flank. Patton was humiliated, but he decided to strike for Palermo. At first he asked permission to take Agrigento, which would give him a harbor for supplies. Alexander approved the maneuver but only if Patton could do it with limited effort. Patton assigned Truscott to reconnoiter Agrigento and told Bradley to forget the road that Montgomery had usurped. Bradley was to sideslip the 45th Infantry Division to the left, across the rear of the 1st Division, and then advance with both divisions to Sicily's northern shore. With Montgomery bogged down on his new route to Messina and with Agrigento captured, Patton flew to North Africa on July 17 to protest his army's support role. An embarrassed Alexander approved a more active role for Patton.[39]

Patton formed a provisional corps under Geoffrey Keyes, his deputy commander, that was composed of the 3rd Infantry and 2nd Armored divisions and pointed it to Palermo. Keyes covered one hundred miles in several days, took three hundred casualties, captured more than fifty thousand Axis prisoners, and seized Palermo on July 22. At the same time, Bradley reached the island's north shore. The action electrified the world while Montgomery was still stalled near Catania, only half-way up the island.

"I feel like a great general today," Patton confided to his diary. He felt the drive to Palermo was the perfect example of the use of armor, and he was pleased to have contributed to it. Driving to the front to visit his advancing troops, he came upon a balking mule, hitched to a cart and blocking a narrow bridge. Patton halted his tanks and then broke his walking stick over the mule driver, had the animal killed, and, to-gether with the cart, pushed off the bridge. The column moved again.[40]

Patton played the part of conquering hero. He met with the cardinal of Sicily and toured the city, which he was happy to discover was less damaged than originally reported. His staff presented him with a Sicil-ian cart, painted with images of his army coming ashore in Gela and himself shaking hands with the cardinal. He took up residence in the city's nine-hundred-year-old royal palace, which contained a grand stair-case and gold furniture. He slept in the king's bedroom on three mat-tresses and ate K rations on fine china adorned with the cross of Saxony. All the palace's servants greeted him with the Nazi salute.[41]

During this time, Patton took an intense interest in German tank technology. He was impressed with the armor added to the German Mark III tank and took pictures of it to send to the Army's Aberdeen Proving Grounds in Maryland for tank designers to study. He was not impressed, however, with Germany's new wonder weapon, the Panzer IV—the Tiger tank that had been first used in North Africa. Patton thought the Tiger "a flop," even though American medium Sherman tanks could not take it out. "They are too slow," he added. He would be proved wrong about the Tigers, especially once the Germans worked the kinks out of the tank and increased its armor.[42]

With Montgomery still stalled on Sicily's eastern face, Patton had an open route to Messina along the northern shore. Meeting Montgomery at his headquarters in Palermo on July 25, Patton was suspicious when the British general ceded him the northern coastal road to Messina as well as a parallel route inland, but Patton was happy to have both. After the meeting, Patton referred to Montgomery as "Montgomery of Palermo," poking fun of the British general's penchant for signing documents "Montgomery of El Alamein." Patton also called himself "Monty's guard of honor" as he escorted the British commander around his headquarters.[43]

Patton focused all his energies on taking Messina before Montgomery. Getting to Messina first would prove that American troops were just as able as the British. Despite pressuring his subordinates, Bradley and Truscott, to move quickly, Patton was unable to make quick progress. The broken Sicilian terrain was hardly helpful.[44]

Patton tried to outflank the enemy. With a small flotilla of landing craft, he put a reinforced battalion behind enemy lines in the early hours of August 8. The men captured a large number of mostly Italian prisoners but failed at anything larger since the Germans were already pulling back to set up another defensive position.[45] Patton ordered another amphibious assault two days later, but Bradley and Truscott, seeing little need to risk lives to prove American mettle and wondering if Patton was out for personal glory, asked him to cancel. Patton refused. Naval officers also objected, but Patton did not listen.[46]

The landing on August 11 put a force of 650 American troops behind the Axis forces. They scurried across the beach and into the high ground, where they set up defensive positions. The Axis forces attacked, and the battle lasted all day. Naval fire, air support, and long-range artillery fire prevented the Germans from overrunning the dug-in positions. Truscott's men finally broke through to the defenders, who compelled the Axis to retreat ahead of schedule. "I have a sixth sense in war . . . and am willing to take chances," Patton wrote in his diary.[47]

Patton ordered another amphibious attack, but it proved unnecessary. Messina was in American hands by 10:00 p.m. on August 16.

Approximately 40,000 Germans and 70,000 Italians had escaped to Italy with 10,000 vehicles, 200 guns, 47 tanks, ammunition, and supplies. Patton drove into the city under Axis fire from the Italian mainland. British forces entered the city from the south the following day. A British officer told Patton, "A jolly good race. I congratulate you."[48]

Patton was pleased. He had fought what he considered to be a close-to-perfect campaign. He proved that Americans were as good as British troops. American losses were relatively light at seven thousand. They had taken one hundred thousand prisoners. Patton was now the most experienced American battle general, but as he stood at the height of his career, his accomplishments would come crashing down.

Patton had slapped two soldiers during the last week of the campaign. Visiting a field hospital in the rear, he worked his way down a row of stretchers offering encouragement to the soldiers. He came upon a man with no bandages and asked where he was hurt. "I guess I can't take it," the soldier responded. Patton burst into rage, cursed him, and slapped his face with his gloves. That evening he sent a memo to his subordinate commanders about men who claimed to be "nervously incapable of combat."

A week later, at another field hospital, Patton was making his way down a line of cots filled with wounded soldiers when he came upon a shivering man. He asked what was wrong. "It's my nerves," the soldier replied and burst into tears. "Your nerves, hell," Patton shouted. "You're just a god-damned coward!" Patton threatened to send the man back to the front or execute him by firing squad. "I ought to shoot you myself right now, goddamn you!" Patton pulled his pistol from its holster, waved it, and struck the man across the face with his other hand. He began to leave but then rushed back and hit the weeping soldier again. A doctor placed himself between Patton and the patient.[49]

Patton did not believe in combat fatigue and thought these men were malingerers. Yet striking an enlisted man was a court-martial offense and could lead to his being relieved of his command. In the heat of a Sicilian summer, close to exhaustion, and frustrated by the enemy's evacuation and escape, Patton lost his balance.

Bradley received a report of the incidents from the doctors and instead of forwarding it, locked it away in his safe. But medical personnel also sent a report directly to Eisenhower.[50] The Supreme Allied Commander dispatched a letter to Patton, castigating him for his actions. Still, Eisenhower had no wish to lose Patton. He met with several senior war correspondents, and they agreed to keep the story buried. Patton, however, would have to apologize. He did so—to Eisenhower to the hospital staff, to the soldiers he had slapped, and, touring the island, to each of his division.

Eisenhower needed Patton for his fighting ability, determination, unflagging aggressiveness, and his refusal to be halted in battle. Eisenhower decided to keep Patton at Army command level, never above, because of his erratic behavior. While Patton remained in Sicily, the war continued. Clark's Fifth Army invaded Italy in September 1943, after taking most of Patton's Seventh Army units. Eisenhower chose Bradley to go to England to begin planning for the cross-channel invasion of France. In evident disgrace and with most of his army gone, Patton had no apparent future.[51]

Patton busied himself with drawing up plans for possible attacks around the Mediterranean. He exercised, read military history, and dined with Italian nobility. He also served in nonexistent invasions as a decoy to deceive the Germans. He traveled to Algiers, Tunis, Corsica, Cairo, Jerusalem, and Malta. In Corsica he visited the house where Napoleon Bonaparte was born; in Jerusalem he saw where Christ was said to have ascended into heaven. He saw the Great Pyramids and the tomb of Ramses II in Egypt. In Malta he visited sixteenth-century forts once occupied by knights who had taken a vow of poverty, chastity, and obedience. "They only kept the last vow," he mentioned in his diary.[52]

On Armistice Day in November, Patton attended a service at a Sicilian cemetery where some of his men were buried. "I consider it no sacrifice," he told the assembly, "to die for my country." That day he turned fifty-eight. He confided to his diary that a year before he had captured Casablanca, "now I command little more than my self-respect."

Later that month, Drew Pearson, a columnist in Washington, D.C., revealed the slapping incidents during a national radio broadcast. The reaction throughout the country was immediate and violent, with calls for Patton's dismissal. Patton was unmoved by the furvor. "I hate and despise slackers and cowards," he told his friends.[53]

The tempest eventually blew over. President Roosevelt, on his way home from the Cairo and Tehran conferences, visited Patton in Sicily. Eisenhower, appointed the Supreme Allied Commander for the invasion of France, told Patton he would probably be transferred to England to participate, although nothing was certain. Feeling useless and discouraged, Patton wondered whether his faith in destiny had deserted him. The series of events physically sickened him. "Send me some more pink medicin [*sic*]," he wrote his wife.[54]

Shattered to learn that Bradley was to command all the American troops in the United Kingdom, Patton felt so low that he spent the next day in bed. "My destiny is sure and I am a fool and a coward even to have doubted it," he penned in his diary on Christmas Day. Yet he was whistling in the dark. It looked as though his services were unwanted.[55]

An odd incident gave Patton a glimmer of hope, the kind that only he could see. While visiting Maj. Gen. Geoffrey Keyes, now the II Corps commander in Italy, Patton, Keyes, and some of their staff officers were walking along a mountain road at the front when Patton stopped, turned to his right, and took a picture of some American artillery guns firing into the German lines. As Patton clicked away, a German artillery barrage came roaring in and exploded on the road thirty feet ahead of him. If Patton had not stopped to take the picture, he would have been walking exactly where the shells hit. Patton's aide, Col. Charles Codman, caught a fragment in his helmet, and the nose of a shell landed inches from Patton's foot. He figured God had spared him for greater deeds. The incident, he wrote, "gives me great confidence."[56]

Finally, word reached Patton on January 22, 1944, to report to Eisenhower in England. He had been saved from disgrace. In England, Patton learned that he would command the U.S. Third Army. Bradley would invade with the U.S. First Army, and then, some time later, he would turn over command to Courtney Hodges, a veteran of World War I, and step up to head the 12th Army Group. Patton's Third Army would then become operational. Montgomery was to be the overall Allied commander of ground troops with a British army and later a Canadian army under him.[57]

Patton set up his Third Army headquarters in Knutsford and purchased a bull terrier he named Willie. He began training his men, as always starting with discipline and military courtesy and then quickly moving to combat proficiency. He traveled constantly to his subordinate units, personally inspecting, teaching, and advising. Suddenly, Eisenhower called Patton to London to replace John Lucas, commander of the VI Corps at Anzio, in Italy. Alexander wanted a "thruster like George Patton," and Patton was happy to have the chance at combat in Italy. Eventually, Truscott was promoted to the VI Corps command, and Patton was no longer needed.[58]

Patton returned to his training regimen with the Third Army. He gave hundreds of speeches to the men. He made them rough and vulgar for the enlisted men and calm and thoughtful for the officers. He encouraged aggressiveness. It was fine to be willing to die for one's country "but a damned sight better to make the German die for his." Mesmerizing his troops, he promised to take the Third Army into Berlin.[59]

In addition to readying the Third Army, Patton served another role. Because of his reputation among the Germans, he commanded a fictitious army group supposedly preparing to invade the continent in the Pas de Calais area. Dummy headquarters, bogus camps, and false radio traffic were all concocted to try to convince the Germans that Patton would lead the invasion in that region, the closest approach to Germany. To lend increased credence to this idea, his name never appeared in the press. Whenever he spoke to troops or civilians, he reminded them that he was a myth, never to be mentioned.[60]

At a newly opened welcome club at Knutsford, Patton said a few words to a small crowd on April 25. He thanked the organizers for furthering the understanding between the British and Americans, who, together with the Russians, were bound to rule the postwar world. The next day, a story of what was called Patton's first public address appeared in the British papers. Apparently, British intelligence wanted to make sure that the Germans knew he was in England. The news was trivial, but the item created a sensation in the United States. Government officials castigated Patton for intruding into politics. Eisenhower was furious. With the invasion only a few months away, he needed no more distractions. Patton again came close to being relieved from duty, but in the end, Eisenhower believed him to be indispensable for the battles ahead.[61]

Normandy and the Battle of the Bulge

P atton flew into a small airstrip near Omaha Beach on July 6 and met with Bradley, Montgomery, and other commanders to get a feel for the fighting. With his army headquarters and troops still funneling into France, he had little to do except visit the troops and tour the Allied front. He was impatient to begin, yet he kept outwardly calm and smiling. He fretted about the situation in his diary, "Neither Ike nor Brad have the stuff."[1]

Patton set up camp in an apple orchard in Nehou south of Cherbourg. He bided his time by supervising experiments with hedgerow-cutting tanks, touring V-1 rocket launch sites, interrogating captured Germans, and flying his Piper Cub airplane. He advised Bradley on operations and played with his dog, Willie.[2]

The Allies were advancing through the hedgerow country of northern France in a slow, bloody campaign in which success was measured in yards. To the east, the British army had captured half of Caen, their D-Day objective. The Germans were putting up a tough fight, and the July rains hampered the Allies. Operation Cobra planned to change all that. Bradley ordered a carpet bombing followed by an infantry and armored assault to break the stalemate and give Patton a chance to exploit it.

The offensive was delayed until July 25 because of the foul weather, but after an unimpressive start, the advance exploded. The bombers had blasted a hole in the German line, and men and tanks charged through. Two days later, as the demoralized Germans retreated, Bradley asked Patton to unofficially take charge of Maj. Gen. Troy Middleton's VIII Corps, which was heading toward Avranches.[3]

Before taking command, Patton and Bradley went aloft in their two Piper Cubs. They flew over the pre-Cobra battle line and witnessed the destruction below. Patton felt like an obvious target but calmed his nerves by taking pictures of the landscape. He considered the bombardment's effects less than the awesome destruction of the World War I battlefields he had witnessed decades before. He also located the spot where his friend Lt. Gen. Leslie McNair was killed days before when American bombs accidentally fell on the American lines. The dead cows below "smelled to high heaven, or at least 300 feet high, as that was my altitude."[4]

Happy to be back in the fight, Patton took command, placing two armored divisions in the van and pointing them to Avranches. It took them only three days to arrive at the town. There they crossed the Pontaubault bridge, giving them access to three directions—west into Brittany, south to the Loire River, and east to the Seine River and Paris. On August 1 Bradley stepped up to command the 12th Army Group and Patton's Third Army was activated. The First Army went to Lt. Gen. Courtney Hodges. The weather cleared, and Patton fed his corps into the battle one at a time through the narrow passage at Avranches. He knew the countryside well from his travels with Beatrice early in his career, and he was right where he needed to be, on the open German flank.[5]

Patton was back in the saddle again, though his name would be kept secret to continue to decoy the Germans into thinking the main invasion was coming at Calais. While the Germans held the other Allied armies in place, Patton's army fanned out. Eisenhower and Bradley made an important decision: instead of sending the whole Third Army into Brittany, they would send only a single corps. Middleton's corps headed west while the other three turned eastward and southward to head for the Seine and Loire rivers.

Patton sent one armored force to Rennes, then Lorient, ten miles away, and another to Brest, two hundred miles distant. Middleton, resigned to the ponderous warfare in the hedgerows, diverted an armored force racing toward Brest to Saint-Malo. Patton, who happened to be traveling to keep a check on his units, found out about Middleton's decision and rescinded it, sending instead an infantry division to Saint- Malo, which fell after three weeks of fighting. The delay gave the Germans time to reinforce Brest, which fell after three weeks of hard fighting by the three divisions. The armored division attacking Lorient had sealed off the Germans in the town, where they would resist capture until the war's end.[6]

Patton next sent his XV Corps, under Maj. Gen. Wade Haislip, and XX Corps, under Maj. Gen. Walton Walker, through the Avranches gap. Both slashed through resistance, bowling over and scattering the Germans. Haislip advanced seventy-five miles to Le Mans. The aggressive action forced a German retreat that Adolf Hitler demanded be stopped. The führer wanted a counterattack. The orders for the German attack, west through Mortain to Avranches, were intercepted and relayed to the Allied commanders via the Ultra code breakers.[7]

On August 7, as Patton's corps slashed east across France, the Germans struck the First Army just north of the Third. But they were quickly brought to a halt with a magnificent defense on the ground, the quick commitment of nearby units, and devastating air attacks. German commanders requested a withdrawal, but Hitler insisted that the operation continue, pushing the lead German units into an Allied noose. To add to the German woes, British forces, led by Canadian troops, broke out of Caen and headed south into the Falaise plain to cut off the attacking Germans.[8]

Patton's superiors, hoping to bag the Germans, ordered him to turn Haislip's corps from a southeastern direction to the north. Patton protested, wanting a deeper penetration, possibly as far as the Seine River, before closing the bag. But the Allied leaders fretted about such a daring plan. The move north was risky enough if the Germans started to retreat and the two American armies would be dangerously far apart. Patton relented and sent Haislip north to take Alençon. On August 13 Haislip closed in on Argentan. The road seemed open, but Patton had already crossed a boundary placed by Montgomery to keep his and Bradley's troops from firing on each other. Bradley ordered Patton to stop at Argentan's outskirts and he obliged.[9]

But the British were not advancing; they were bogged down north of Falaise. Bradley waited in vain for Montgomery's invitation to head north and meet the Canadians above Falaise and close the noose. Unhappy with Bradley's complacency, Patton requested that he be allowed to continue east to attempt his larger encirclement. On August 14, with Bradley's blessing, Patton sent three corps charging east to Dreux, Chartres, and Orléans, well into the interior of northern France. Two days later they had all reached their destinations. Patton called it "probably the fastest and biggest pursuit in history." He was right: no American army had ever moved with such speed and dash. As a reward, Eisenhower released Patton's name to the press the next day, giving him credit for the breakout.[10]

On August 15 the Allies landed in southern France. The next day, Hitler permitted the forces in the Falaise pocket to withdraw. At the same time, Canadian forces reached Falaise and Montgomery asked Bradley to move his forces up to meet with his to close the pocket. No one was on the scene to conduct the maneuver for the Third Army, so Patton sent back Hugh Gaffey with a provisional headquarters to begin the attack. Simultaneously, Bradley sent Leonard Gerow to the area to do the same. As Gaffey prepared an attack, Gerow arrived and, disliking Gaffey's plan, began putting together his own offensive, which he launched on August 18, giving the Germans another day to flee.[11]

Although the Canadians and Americans made a tenuous link on August 19, they were not able to secure the pocket until August 21. They met in the town of Chambois, roughly halfway between Falaise and Argentan. The Germans lost about fifty thousand men, but another one hundred thousand soldiers escaped. Bradley's delays gave the Germans an additional five days to flee. If Patton had been allowed to head north as he originally requested, the Allies might have captured or destroyed the German army in the west. Eisenhower, Bradley, and Montgomery did not have Patton's determination, willingness to take great risks, or confidence in their men. They could not accomplish the feat of destroying two German armies.

Meanwhile, Patton sent Haislip to Mantes, thirty miles from Paris. He wanted to send two of Haislip's divisions across the Seine River to prevent a German crossing, but again his superiors deemed the action too risky. He was allowed to send one across and the other to the left bank in an ineffective attempt to block the exit. The Germans had escaped and would come back to haunt the Western Allies again in four months. Paris was freed, and although the headlines trumpeted Patton's liberation of the City of Lights, Hodges's First Army that first entered the city.[12]

When the commander of Patton's XII Corps, Maj. Gen. Gilbert Cook, became too ill to command, Patton replaced him with Manton Eddy, whose 9th Infantry Division had performed well in Sicily and had cut off the Cherbourg Peninsula. Eddy was an infantryman, not used to the slashing tactics of his commander, Patton. When Eddy asked Patton how much he should worry about his flanks when on the attack, Patton told him it depended on how nervous he was. When Eddy told Patton he thought progressing a mile a day was good going, Patton told him to go fifty miles. Eddy, according to Patton, turned pale but he soon accomplished the request.[13]

Patton attacked east, covering seventy miles in a single day, and crossed the Seine River before the Germans could destroy the bridges. He continued east, well past Paris, to the battlefields where he had fought in World War I. Troyes, Reims, and Châlons-en-Champagne fell quickly. German resistance in France was crumbling. Patton hoped to get across the Moselle River between Nancy and Metz but was stopped cold—though not by the Germans. Patton's swift advance outdistanced the supplies that were still being off-loaded on the Normandy beaches. Even the Red Ball Express, a convoy of trucks racing to get supplies to the fighting units, could not keep up with the Allies' progress. Patton's attack sputtered to a halt, advancing as far as the Meuse River, which he crossed on August 31.[14]

Patton was tantalizingly close to the Siegfried line, the unmanned German border defenses. He begged Bradley for four hundred thousand gallons of fuel, promising to be in Germany in two days, but no fuel was available. Eisenhower had decided to support Montgomery's advance in the north, which was aimed at the port of Antwerp and the German V-1 and V-2 missile launch sites.[15]

Frustrated by the turn of events, Patton managed to keep an outward expression of cheerfulness. He wrote his wife, telling her, "God deliver us from our friends, we can handle the enemy." To make matters worse, rain and winter weather came early to Western Europe. By the time his army was replenished, it was too late to recapture its momentum. German resistance stiffened and Patton's new advance slowed to a crawl. Those three events—improved German resistance, worsening weather conditions, and a lack of fuel—combined with an end to the open rolling countryside of western France, changed the nature of the Third Army's war.

While Nancy fell on September 15, Metz, fortified by World War I defenses, held out until mid-November. Patton was forced to transfer one of his corps to Lt. Gen. Jacob Devers, whose 6th Army Group had joined the race to the German border. In addition, Patton had to yield supplies to Montgomery's Operation Market Garden, an ill-fated attempt to cross the Rhine in Holland. Patton was forced to go on the defensive.[16]

Patton spent his time enthusiastically visiting his army units. As he had in North Africa, he made sure mail was delivered, the food was as good as it could be, and the proper clothing was sent to the frontline men. Units were rotated off of the line, and passes were granted. He crossed the Moselle himself in mid-September and visited the front lines, crawling into a muddy observation post to watch a nearby tank battle. He was impressed that he could hear the different rates of fire between the American and German tanks.[17]

He came under fire often during the push to Germany. In late September, while returning to the front, a shell burst showered his Jeep with mud. A second shell came even closer, about eight feet from the Jeep. "Luckily this shell was a dud or these lines would not be written," he penned to his wife. His closest call may have come on October 24, when the Germans fired a 280 mm rail gun at his house in Nancy. Two shells exploded thirty feet from the house, demolishing another home. The blast shattered Patton's windows. He ran outside and helped pull an old man and a little boy from the wreckage.[18] At the end of October Bradley visited him and told him he could go on the attack again. "I feel 40 years younger," he wrote Bea.[19]

Patton planned his attack for November 8 with ten divisions. As the date drew near, he developed a case of shortness of breath—his usual reaction to an upcoming fight. He also developed indigestion and vomiting, but he still was ready to move forward with the battle. The night before the attack, as the rains poured, several of his commanders begged him to postpone the attack and wait for better weather. Patton refused. When he went to bed that night, he was too anxious to sleep. He started reading Rommel's book on World War I infantry attacks, picking out a section at random that happened to be about fighting in the rain in September 1914. Patton took it as a sign from heaven that he was doing the right thing. When he awoke to the sounds of Third Army's artillery he noticed that the rains had stopped.[20]

Patton went to the front to watch the attack with Eddy. As usual, his visit was brief; he did not like to hang around his commanders during a battle, believing it showed a lack of faith in their leadership. While standing on a hill with Eddy, both using binoculars to watch the battle, Patton impressed one of Eddy's aides. Brig. Gen. Eric Wood recorded that a decision from Patton was needed: "He stood . . . without moving, looking into space for perhaps three minutes. Then he turned to General Eddy and gave his decision, leaving the O.P. (observation post) immediately thereafter.[21]"

The good opening did not last. By nightfall the rains returned and poured on Patton's men as they tried to break the German lines. The "liquid mud" and stiff German resistance made Third Army's advance incremental. Farther north, Walton Walker, the commander of XX Corps, unleashed some two thousand bombers on the Metz force, shaking the ground under Patton's feet as he watched the destruction. But to his rear, almost all of the bridges over the Moselle were washed out. Despite the floods, Patton was optimistic: "They hurt the Germans worse than they do us because they cannot get away from us, and I am quite sure we are killing a large number of them."[22]

Even though the battle was joined, Patton still had time to correct minor problems for his troops' benefit. When he went to Sunday Mass and "heard the worst service yet," he had the chaplain replaced. He checked on cases of immersion foot among the frontline soldiers and issued a memorandum on prevention to his corps and division commanders. He also traveled to the lines to work out problems. In dark and rainy Thionville, Patton came across a military policeman who was having trouble keeping vehicles spaced apart as they crossed a newly erected bridge over the Moselle. Patton offered to help, and the MP, not realizing who he was talking to, agreed. Patton immediately walked up to a Jeep near the bridge and chewed out the officer in the passenger seat for covering up his rank—a practice many officers followed to prevent German snipers from singling them out from their soldiers. Patton rejected the practice and threatened to make the officer a private. He then ordered the officer to start spacing his vehicles. "It took about 10 minutes for things to get better," the MP recorded.[23]

By November 19 Third Army had surrounded Metz and street fighting had ensued. A German general in the city sent a message to the Americans that his men would fight to the death. "We are trying to satisfy him," Patton wrote. Three days later the city officially fell, though several forts still held out. A captured SS major general was brought to Patton, who asked his captive why, "if he wanted to be a good Nazi" he did not commit suicide? In his defense, the general declared himself a prisoner of the American Army. Patton threatened to turn him over to the French army, saying, "They can do things I can't do." He sent him away, telling his interpreter to remind the prisoner "that those bayonets on the guards' guns are very sharp." To celebrate the liberation of Metz and Nancy, Patton had his guard of honor play three ruffles and three flourishes for Walker and Eddy. The series of three was usually reserved for lieutenant generals. "I hope this is prophetic," Patton commented.[24]

As he pushed forward, losing men and realizing no replacements were on the way, Patton combed rear areas for any troops, including staff officers; gave them some training; and put them on the front lines. On his birthday, while at the front "getting where the dead were still warm," he discovered that Devers had reached the Rhine River, "making a monkey out of me."[25]

The campaign was affecting Patton's commanders. Most of his corps commanders had problems with their division commanders. The worst case was between Eddy and Jack Wood, the commander of the 4th Armored Division. Wood, used to the same slashing tactics as Patton, frequently clashed with the more cautious Eddy. Wood had raced for

Avranches and broken into Brittany. He had also spearheaded Third Army's attack across France. He was considered by some to be a better tank commander than even Patton, but that did not excuse insubordination. In early December, Wood lost his temper in the presence of Eddy and his staff. Patton should have sent him home in disgrace, but Wood's contributions to the war had been so great and Patton considered him a friend. Wood was instead sent home for sixty days' detached service. The official word was that he had become "too nervous."[26]

On December 2 Patton went forward to look at the Saar River—on France's border with Germany—in a house used as an observation post. Although the regimental commander suggested that Patton approach the house through an apple orchard, Patton refused and took an open road. Once Patton was in the house and observing the other side of the river, Germans nearby opened up with everything they had. Patton and his party stormed out of the house, through the apple orchard, and away from the enemy fire, leaving everyone wet and covered in mud.

By December 15 Third Army had advanced thirty-five to forty miles in heavy fighting and was preparing a final attack. The last fort of isolated Metz had fallen three days earlier. Patton had crossed the Moselle and Saar rivers and was now in Germany with his sights set on the Rhine. Despite his problems, he was optimistic; "everyone has lost faith in me but me." That was about to change.

During the November battles, Patton had noticed that the First and Ninth armies were fighting on narrower fronts than his. He commented, "The First Army is making a terrible mistake in leaving the VIII Corps static, as it is highly probably that the Germans are building up east of them." Patton's sixth sense for war was validated when his G-2, Oscar Koch, told him on December 9 that he thought the Germans were concentrating their forces on the VIII Corps' front, even though none of the Allied intelligence agreed with him. Patton began planning for a possible relief of the forces to his north. He was right. The Germans were harboring their forces opposite of the First Army, preparing for Hitler's last gamble to win the war, the Battle of the Bulge.[27]

On December 16 the Germans struck though the Ardennes Forest with three armies, hoping to split the British and American armies, capture Antwerp, and destroy the Western Allies piecemeal. The American

106th Infantry Division lost two of its three regiments, St. Vith fell after a hard fight, and Bastogne, where the 101st Airborne Division had been rushed to stem the German tide, would soon be surrounded. Patton, preparing an offensive of his own, took a call from Bradley, who ordered him to transfer his 10th Armored Division to Hodges. Patton complained, but as he hung up the phone, he turned to his aide, Col. Charles Codman, and said, "I guess they're having trouble up there. I thought they would."[28]

Patton met with Bradley on December 18 to assess the situation. He said he was surprised by the Germans' progress. Bradley asked him what he could do, and Patton responded that he could attack at once, sending one division north at midnight, one at first light, and one in twenty-four hours. He might also be able to move another corps north if Devers could extend his own front to the north. If Bradley gave the word, he would change the direction of an entire army from east to north, a confusing and dangerous maneuver if not handled deftly. Not only would Patton be changing the orientation of his fighting men, he would be changing the direction of supplies and replacements, all over icy roads in freezing temperatures. Bradley asked Patton to be in Verdun the next day for a meeting with Eisenhower.

Patton immediately phoned his chief of staff and began giving orders. He wanted two divisions stopped and realigned under a new corps. He also wanted all the transportation Third Army could muster to move infantry units north. Early the next morning, he held a meeting with his corps and division commanders to work out the different plans of attack. He arranged a simple series of code words so he could telephone after the Verdun meeting and use one word to determine the thrust of his attack.

At Verdun, Patton arrived to find Bradley, Eisenhower, Devers, and their staffs already there. After a rather gloomy assessment of the situation by Eisenhower's G-2, Eisenhower spoke up: "The present situation is to be regarded as one of opportunity for us and not of disaster." Patton added to Eisenhower's optimism, saying, "Hell, let's have the guts to let the bastards go all the way to Paris, then we'll really cut them off and chew them up." Laughter broke out; the tension was eased.[29]

When Eisenhower asked when Patton could attack, Patton did not miss a beat: "On December 22, with three divisions." Everyone was astonished. How could anyone pull off an attack with such speed? Unflapped, Eisenhower questioned the size of the force, thinking three divisions was too small an effort for a strong blow against the enemy. Patton defended the plan, reasoning it was better to strike immediately with three divisions than to wait for more and forfeit the element of surprise. Eisenhower agreed, and Patton called his headquarters to relay the proper code words for the attack.[30]

The next day, Patton met again with Bradley in Luxembourg City to discuss the situation. Patton had moved his headquarters there to better coordinate his maneuver. He proposed a drive to the northeast, cutting off the German bulge at its base. Bradley countered that the attack should commence farther west to relieve Bastogne, where the 101st Airborne continued to hold out against the Germans. Patton agreed.

Patton spent the next day shifting units. Hundreds of tanks and vehicles, hospitals, depots, and other elements that compose an army had to be moved, and Patton directed it all by telephone. He managed to visit seven of his divisions in one day. On December 22 three divisions under the newly arrived III Corps commander, John Millikin, began their advance along a twenty-mile front. Despite heavy snows, rough terrain, and enemy resistance, the troops made seven miles on their first day. Farther north, Anthony McAuliffe, the temporary commander of the 101st in surrounded Bastogne, responded to a German surrender request with one word: "Nuts!"[31]

Patton insisted on day and night attacks for his 4th Armored Division. Even though the division progressed five miles the next day, it ran into heavy German forces on Christmas Eve and was pushed back. Patton blamed himself for the setback, but at least the weather began to clear, giving Allied airpower a crack at the exposed German columns heading west. Also on that day, Patton sent out a holiday message to all units in the Third Army, expressing confidence "in your courage, devotion to duty, and skill in battle." Included in the message was a prayer to "restrain these immoderate rains." It had been composed before the rain had turned into snow.

Millikin's corps continued pushing north, with Patton showing up everywhere along the line to encourage soldiers and help to keep the columns moving. He crossed the Sure River, the only natural obstacle south of Bastogne, on a hastily built footbridge, stepping over dead bodies along the way. He was able to find time to attend a Christmas service in Luxembourg, sitting in the same pew as Kaiser Wilhelm had during World War I.[32]

Later that day, at a meeting with Bradley, Patton learned that Montgomery was suggesting a halt for all of the Allies. Monty had taken command of the American First Army because he was in the best position geographically to do so. Eisenhower had not wanted Bradley to risk traveling to the First Army because the Germans had blocked his route. Instead, he put the army under the temporary command of Monty until the crisis passed. Monty claimed that the First Army would not be ready to go on the offensive for another three months and Patton's Third Army was too weak to attack. The suggestions infuriated Patton, whose divisions were closing in on Bastogne. "If ordered to fall back, I think I will ask to be relieved," he confided to his diary.[33]

Finally, as the sun began to set on December 26, tanks of the 4th Armored Division crashed through the German defenses around Bastogne and relieved the town. Although it would take a few days to strengthen the corridor Patton had established, the Germans were spent. Patton considered the relief of Bastogne his most brilliant operation and outstanding achievement of the war.[34]

But the battle was not over. With Bastogne relieved, Patton continued north to close the bulge. On December 30 he sent an armored division and an infantry division that were west of Bastogne on an eastward attack and caught the flank of a German thrust at the town, stopping it cold. Later that day Patton drove into the town to award medals to some of the town's defenders. He drove through an artillery barrage, passing buttoned-up tanks along the way and inspiring the men who saw him. "They were delighted and wanted me to drive slowly so the soldiers could see me.[35]

On January 3 First Army began heading south to Houffalize, where it would meet Patton's Third and close the bulge. But Patton was not directing his entire army north. Instead he attacked a pocket of heavy German resistance southeast of Bastogne. Patton's entire force now consisted of seventeen divisions, and he was confident of the outcome. "It has been a very violent battle under appalling weather conditions, but we are going to win."[36]

Patton now worried about the Germans escaping the bag. When the Germans launched counterattacks against his thrusts, he saw them as more evidence of a German withdrawal. On January 9 he had Eddy's XII Corps attack north from Diekirch, east of Bastogne, ignoring Eddy's protests that his left flank was exposed. To support the attack, Patton had Middleton's VIII Corps, west of Bastogne, attack north. Middleton also complained that his men were spent, but Patton held his ground and ordered the attack to proceed. On learning that the Germans planned to strike his army to the south and retake Metz, he ordered Walker's XX Corps to prepare any bridges for demolition. "Again, I earned my pay."[37]

When the Germans attacked farther south, it was against Alexander Patch's Seventh Army. Eisenhower wanted any advances toward Houffalize stopped and reinforcements sent to XX Corps. Patton agreed, but had misgivings. But with Bradley's approval, he sent his reinforcements into reserve, where they could travel either south or north, wherever needed. Patton was not happy about the situation. "This is the second time I have been stopped in a successful attack due to the Germans having more nerve than we have," he confessed to his diary.

Patton pushed his men relentlessly to keep attacking, fearing, correctly, that the Germans were escaping eastward. He blamed Eisenhower and Montgomery for not pursuing the enemy with the same abandon. When he came across a truck stalled in the snow, he ordered the men out to push, putting his own shoulder into the effort. He chewed out any leader who allowed the attack to stall. No one understood more than Patton the need for speed.

No chance to share his fiery style of leadership was ever wasted. In one instance, Patton drove by a group of tired infantrymen resting along the side of a road while their officers conferred. Patton, sitting in the passenger seat of his Jeep behind a hood-mounted machine gun, got out and approached the men. "Man!" he exclaimed, "Von Runstedt's nuts are in a meat grinder and I've got the handle in my hand." He then smiled and returned the men's salutes with a wave of his hand before getting back in the Jeep and speeding away.[38]

To Patton, the weather was "a greater menace than the enemy." The temperatures dropped below zero, snow drifts blinded soldiers, and tanks slid off of icy roads. "It is amazing that men can exist, much less fight, in such weather." He himself was not immune to the weather. After spending an entire day in an open command car, he awoke the next morning to find his eyes swollen shut and "running like a spigot." A doctor treated him with cold compresses, and he was soon back to work.[39]

On January 16 elements of Third Army linked with First Army in Houffalize, effectively cutting off the bulge. Patton wrote his son about the victory, accounting for some eighty thousand Germans. "The woods are full of corpses, and it is going to stink some in the spring," he wrote. Patton's greatest campaign had come to an end.[40] He spent the rest of January eliminating the remaining Germans in the pocket and chasing them out of Belgium and Luxembourg.

The End of the War and Occupation

With the Battle of the Bulge over, Patton continued his pursuit of the German army. But in early February Eisenhower assigned Montgomery the main effort to push to the Rhine River, the last natural barrier to Germany. Bradley threatened to quit when he wasn't chosen, and Patton told him, "I will lead the procession." Reduced to a defensive position, Patton considered the order "a foolish and ignoble way for the Americans to end the war."[1] Patton would have none of it. He pushed his commanders to keep gaining ground but flooded rivers, muddy roads, and stiff German resistance from the Siegfried line slowed his progress.

Patton crossed the Sauer River into Germany on February 13, 1945, in true warrior fashion: mortars firing on either side of his vehicle, a smoke screen drifting across the river, and artillery shells exploding all around. Once across, he toured the Siegfried line, which had held his army up for so long. He was not impressed. He considered the dragon's teeth, cement pylons designed to stop tanks, "a useless form of amusement," and the line in general built by "gullible fools."[2] He now set his sights on one thing: the Rhine River.

Making steady progress but unable to break out in the rainy weather, Patton headed to Paris, where he bought silverware, hunted pheasant, and took in a show at the Follies Bergère. When he entered his box at the theater, he received a standing ovation. Returning to the front three days later, he relished the newspaper clippings about his progress.

On his return to Germany, Patton visited the front lines. While inspecting his 94th Infantry Division, he entered a house opposite a German strong point. As the door closed behind him, German machine-gun rounds exploded through the door, about a foot away from him. He looked at the door, then at the soldiers in the house, and said, "That was close, wasn't it?" When told where the officer he was looking for was, he turned and walked out the same door.[3]

Patton called Bradley to ask for an armored division, but he was not in and a staffer permitted the release of the 10th Armored Division to Third Army. Patton put the division to use immediately, spearheading an attack on the German city of Trier. As the division, supported by an infantry division, neared the city, Bradley told Patton to bypass the city, since it would take four divisions to capture it. Patton responded the next day that he had taken Trier with two divisions. "What do you want me to do? Give it back?" Patton visited the ancient city and toured its Roman amphitheater, commenting that he could "smell the sweat of the legions."[4]

On March 7 the Third Army reached the Rhine—quite a feat considering the river was much farther east in Germany than it was in the British and First Army zones. On that same day, armored infantrymen of the First Army captured a bridge across the Rhine intact at Remagen. Patton was jealous of Courtney Hodges's luck, but he was happy the Americans made it across before the British did.[5]

Without a bridge to cross, Patton focused on bringing his whole army along the river. When Eisenhower visited in mid-March, the two stayed up until 2:30 in the morning talking. They were still great friends, though Patton harbored resentment at Eisenhower's lack of praise, his humiliating punishments for the slapping incidents and the Knutsford affair, as well as what he perceived to be Ike's timidity on the battlefield.[6]

If anyone appreciated Patton, it was the Germans. A captured German lieutenant colonel confessed during an interrogation that the Third Army was Germany's biggest threat and that Patton was always the main topic of military meetings, especially since the Battle of the Bulge. He added that Patton was "the most feared general on all fronts" and that Third Army's success overshadowed all events, "including the campaign in Russia."[7]

While driving to the front, Patton and his caravan passed what he considered "one of the greatest scenes of destruction I have ever witnessed." Near the town of Neustadt, destroyed German vehicles, weapons, and, "I am sorry to say, dead horses" littered the road. Elements of the 10th Armored Division caught up with a retreating German column and drove up next to it before opening fire. Some of the fighting occurred less than ten feet away. Most of the German vehicles were forced into a gully along the side of the road. "A tanker's dream come true," Patton cheered.[8]

During the night of March 22, using surprise and speed, Patton slipped a division across the Rhine—an entire day before Montgomery's much ballyhooed and elaborate crossing farther north. Patton was ecstatic. "This operation is stupendous," he wrote Bea. He praised his soldiers, reminding them that crossing the Rhine "assures you of even greater glory to come." Accolades came rolling in. Eisenhower wrote Patton with a "deep appreciation" for Third Army's deeds. The chief of staff, George Marshall, wrote the general a personal note of appreciation, and Secretary of War Henry Stimson wrote, "We gave Monty everything he asked for—paratroops, assault boats, and even the Navy, and by God! Patton has crossed the Rhine."[9]

To celebrate, Patton drove onto a pontoon bridge spanning the river, stopped in the middle, got out of his car, and urinated into the river. "The pause that refreshes," he called it. As he stepped ashore on the far bank, he fell deliberately to the ground, and as he stood up, grabbed two fistfuls of soil and said, "And thus, William the Conqueror!" He was reenacting William's similar fall when he landed in England and said, "I have taken England with both hands."[10]

As the Third Army penetrated deeper into Germany, Patton thought more and more about his son-in-law, John Waters, who had been captured in North Africa. Patton was getting close to the prisoner of war camp in Hammelburg, where Waters was thought to be, and he wanted to arrive there before the prisoners could be moved deeper into the heart of Germany. This maneuver would be as controversial as any of his other personal blunders.

Patton discussed the matter with Manton Eddy, who was attacking north, not east in the direction of the camp. They decided to form a task force under Capt. Abe Baum, comprised of three hundred men with ten medium tanks, six light tanks, twenty-seven half-tracks, seven Jeeps, and three motorized assault guns. The mission was to smash through the German front line, drive forty miles to Hammelburg, enter the camp, and rescue the prisoners. Along for the trip was Al Stiller, one of Patton's aides, who could recognize Waters. Stiller's presence later fueled suspicion about the task force's true mission. Was it to liberate the prisoners or retrieve Waters?

In the darkness of March 26, the task force burst through the German lines and headed for Hammelburg. The Germans at first thought this was Third Army's main attack, but daylight revealed the force's small size. A German officer who had been captured to act as a guide for the task force was released, and he immediately reported its destination to his superiors. Baum made it to the camp, only to discover more prisoners than expected. Waters was wounded in the confusion of the liberation and was forced to stay. By the time Baum had loaded as many prisoners as he could into the half-tracks, the Germans were ready for him. His troops were surrounded, and he was forced to surrender at sunrise the next morning.[11]

The operation was a disaster. Not only was the task force too small for its mission, but Patton also failed to assign it any air cover. Only a single observation plane flew overhead to call in artillery support for the first leg of the drive. A few prisoners who had fled on foot eventually made it through enemy lines to report what had happened. Fortunately, when Bradley and Eisenhower found out about the raid, they kept it quiet.[12]

The Seventh Army liberated the camp nine days later, and Waters was flown to a hospital in Frankfort, where Patton visited him. When Waters asked Patton if he knew he was in the camp, Patton answered, "Not for sure." Waters was emaciated and weak, but Patton wrote his wife that a blood transfusion and a meal returned him to shape. "His spirit is unbroken." Patton never spoke about the incident again as newspapers blamed him for sacrificing men for his son-in-law. "How I hate the press," he wrote Beatrice.[13]

Patton saw the pursuit into Germany as a footrace with the other Allied armies, but Eisenhower, mindful of the Russians, kept his armies even with each other. Patton detested Eisenhower's seeming timidity. "Had a bold policy throughout been used in this war, it would have long since been over."[14]

The soldiers of the Third Army were the first to discover Hitler's greatest atrocity when they liberated the infamous Ohrdruf Nord concentration camp. Eisenhower and Bradley accompanied Patton to what he called "one of the most appalling sights I have ever seen." The camp confirmed the worst rumors about death camps in Germany. So disgusted was Patton that he had the town mayor and his wife escorted through the camp. On their return home from the visit, they hanged themselves. Eisenhower, Bradley, and Patton ordered the townspeople to tour the camp. Later, when Third Army liberated Buchenwald, a much worse concentration camp, Patton threw up during his inspection.[15]

In April Patton found out Berlin was out of the picture for the Western Allies. In frustration, he drove to Bradley's headquarters to confront the general on what he perceived to be an unfair strategy. "Brad," he asked, "why in hell are you calling me back? I've got the Boche on the run and I can surround Berlin and capture the whole German army if you would let me go!" Bradley patiently replied that they were not his orders but rather came down from Roosevelt and Churchill. Patton cried.[16] Actually, Eisenhower had agreed to let the Russians capture the German capital while the Allies concentrated on the suspected German redoubt along the Austro-Hungarian border. Patton felt cheated out of the prize, predicting, correctly, that the redoubt was merely the creation of Nazi propaganda.

Patton responded to the disappointment by flying to Paris again for a short break. On his first morning at breakfast in the City of Light, his friend Everett Hughes noticed in *Stars and Stripes* that Patton had been promoted to full general. He passed the paper to Patton, who scanned the page and threw the paper down. Hughes retrieved it and gave it back to Patton, who put it down again. Finally, Hughes handed him the paper again, pointing out the story and saying, "Read that." Patton did, then leaned back, and in a loud voice said, "Well, I'll be god-dammed." He had been expecting the promotion.[17]

Patton returned to the front and, while flying between his corps headquarters, was fired on by a British Spitfire fighter with Polish markings. Patton's pilot took evasive action and descended. The Spitfire came around again, machine guns blasting. It made a third pass, but the Polish pilot could not pull out of the dive and crashed. Throughout it all, Patton tried to take pictures of the action but was so rattled by the attack he had forgotten to take the lens cap off his camera.[18]

The Spitfire incident was not Patton's last brush with death. In May he narrowly missed being skewered by a pole on a bull cart that careened down a side street in a small German town. The pole missed him by only a few inches. Were the Spitfire and cart incidents signs of Patton's coming death?

Third Army's last mission was to head for Czechoslovakia. Crossing the Danube River at Regensburg, Patton told his aide, Charles Codman, that he had been with Napoleon for the storming of the town centuries before. Patton did not think the Danube very blue, but he was impressed with its swiftness. As he crossed he noticed in the distance "some kind of Nazi shrine." It turned out to be Valhalla, a memorial to famous Germans built in the early 1800s. Patton would later visit the hall and have his picture taken as one of the Greats of Germany. He even had Willie pose for a victory picture.[19]

Patton ordered Clarence Huebner's V Corps to attack no farther than Pilsen. Huebner reached the town easily and asked Patton if he could go for Prague, where patriots had risen up against their German occupiers and were asking the Western Allies for help. Patton contacted Bradley. Bradley put the question to Eisenhower. The answer came back no; Prague had also been reserved for the Russians. Patton hated that he had been denied another of Europe's great capitals.[20]

Germany formally surrendered on May 9, 1945, in a ceremony signed in Reims, France, Eisenhower's headquarters, and later in Berlin. Patton predicted "a tremendous letdown." He spent the day at the Skoda Munitions Plant in Pilsen, taking pictures of German tank bogie wheels he thought were good for light tanks. Had he fulfilled his destiny? Was there nothing more for him?

Patton had had his eye on the Pacific theater since February, when he volunteered to fight under MacArthur, who ignored the request, obviously not wanting to share the spotlight with the famous Patton. MacArthur did accept Bradley and Hodges. Undaunted, Patton wrote Gen. George C. Marshall about a command fighting the Japanese, explaining, "I am of such an age that this war will be my last war, and I would like to see it though to the end." Marshall promised Patton a command in China, but only if the Chinese captured a port from the Japanese, which was not likely. Patton even wrote his friend Robert Eichelberger, the commander of the Eighth Army under MacArthur, and offered to sit at his feet and learn Pacific warfare. Eichelberger could not make any promises.

Patton set up headquarters in a former Nazi Youth complex in Bad Tölz in Bavaria. He resided in a modern villa with a swimming pool and a boathouse. He furnished his office with a desk previously used by Rommel. "If one has to occupy Germany," he mused, "this is a good place to do it from." He toured Berlin, which he had visited in 1912 after the Olympics, and found it depressing. He decided that the Allies had destroyed a "good race," only to replace it with "Mongolian savages."[21]

Although the war was over in Europe, Patton could envision another one right around the corner. He detested the Russians and predicted a war with the Soviet Union, which he thought it best to start while the U.S. Army's strength was at its peak. But he knew his idea was out of the question. The Soviet Union was still a U.S. ally in the war against Japan, and the American people would not accept such a sacrifice at the end of a war as bloody as World War II. He sympathized with German refugees, though, and turned a blind eye to the thousands who crossed his border, fleeing Russian occupiers.

Patton went from leading a campaigning army to overseeing an army of occupation. He took over northern Germany, hardly a glorious accolade for America's greatest battlefield commander. The day after the German surrender, he was called to a meeting with Eisenhower along with the top American commanders. Eisenhower told them the importance of presenting a united front in case they were called to testify before a congressional committee on the war's conduct. Patton sensed that Eisenhower was trying to cover up "probable criticism of strategical blunders which he unquestionably committed during the campaign."[22]

As Patton saw it, Germany's destruction created a power vacuum in Europe. The French were too weak and the British too untrusting. The Russians, whom Patton called Mongols, threatened the postwar peace. "They are a scurvy race and simply savages. We could beat the hell out of them." The only logical choice for an ally against Russia was Germany, whose troops had fought nobly on the battlefield and knew something about the Soviet Union, where the next war would inevitably be. Patton argued that people should forget about Nazi excesses and be generous to their defeated enemy, much as Abraham Lincoln had hoped the North would be to the South after the American Civil War. The Nazi Party was just like the Republican or Democratic parties, he told a press conference: some Germans had joined the party merely to advance their careers. Patton thought the key to fulfilling his destiny lay with Germany becoming an ally.[23]

In mid-May Patton flew to Paris and then London for a short vacation. He wanted to return to Knutsford to visit friends there, but before he could leave for London, Eisenhower called him to Reims. On arriving at Eisenhower's headquarters, Patton learned that Tito, the communist maverick who had fought the Germans in a guerrilla war, was now "raising hell" in what would become Yugoslavia. Marshall had recommended sending Patton at the head of five armored divisions to bluff Tito, but the communist leader soon backed down. For Patton, it was a moment of excitement in the mundane postwar world, but with plans terminated, he set off for England as planned.[24]

In early June Patton flew home to a hero's welcome. Landing outside Boston, he greeted Beatrice for the first time since 1942. Having grown frail while he was away, she looked older, grayer, and smaller to him. His son George IV in his West Point uniform was also there to meet him. A million Bostonians turned out to cheer Patton as he rode in an open car, standing to receive his accolades on his way to the city's Hatch Memorial Shell, an open-air theater (where a statue of him now stands). Once there, he gave a speech that undercut his triumph. He told the crowd that a soldier killed in combat was not necessarily a hero but frequently a fool. He pointed to the four hundred wounded soldiers of the Third Army, who were seated in a special section. "These men are the heroes," he told the crowd and saluted them.[25]

Patton was attempting to pay tribute to the men returning home and those who were still fighting the Japanese, but his words struck a raw nerve with Gold Star parents whose sons gave their lives for their country. The widely publicized speech prompted some to write Marshall and Secretary of War Stimson, complaining that Patton had besmirched the names of the men who lay buried in the military cemeteries across the world. The Army Public Relations Bureau sent out stories and answered letters trying to explain Patton's meaning.

After a few days in and around Boston, Patton flew to Denver and then Los Angeles, where one hundred thousand people turned out to hear him. At every speech, Patton talked about defeating Japan, his impressions of the home front, and Third Army's triumphs. He ran the gamut of emotions, laughing and crying as he spoke or listened to others. After a few days in California, it was off to Fort Riley, Kansas, and then to Washington, D.C., where he visited his daughters and grandchildren. While visiting a double-amputee ward at Walter Reed Medical Center, he burst into tears. "God damn it," he cried. "If I had been a better general, most of you wouldn't be here."[26]

By the end of his trip, Patton was mentally spent. The postwar world was alien to him, and he was uncomfortable in the civilian world, where people were glad the war was almost over. Before he left Washington, he told his daughters that he had foreseen his own death and that they would never again see him alive. When they tried to argue with him he cut them off, so sure was he of his premonition.

He wanted to get back to his command, where life made sense, and his return to Europe was everything he expected. He flew into Bavaria escorted by three fighter groups and was greeted by an honor guard and a band. He passed through rows of tanks and soldiers in a car flanked by motorcycles while planes flew over. This was where he wanted to be. Instead of administering his region of responsibility, Patton spent his time visiting his troops. He missed war. People around him noticed that he looked older, that the old fire was gone. Without combat he seemed to lose his focus, he seemed out of touch with events. When Japan surrendered he worried to his wife that "the horrors of peace, pacifism and unions will have unlimited sway."[27]

His gloom began to overwhelm him, poisoning his mind. He questioned how the war had ended, why he had been denied Berlin. He worried about Bolshevik power, Europe's future, and Germany's fate. He saw labor leaders, communists, and Jews conspiring against the United States. Unable to suppress his own prejudices, he lapsed into the neurotic comfort of stereotyping. The imprisoned peoples of Germany, who were now free, were nothing but labor leaders, Jews, and communists. The physical and mental fatigue of leading men in battle for almost three years had robbed him of his equilibrium. "I think I was never so tired and stiff as I was yesterday," he wrote his wife.[28]

Patton's paranoia and prejudices were having an effect on his professional responsibilities. When criticized for his lackadaisical attitude toward denazification, he said that he never knew the war was fought to denazify Germany. "Live and Learn," he wrote. He saw only a weak Germany getting weaker so that the Russians could dominate it. Patton had missed the war's entire point: to rid the world of a ruthless tyrant. He forgot about the extermination camps and saw the Germans as ordinary people who had fought honorably. The real troublemakers had to be the Jews, he reasoned, who wanted only revenge and who spread their opinions in newspapers.[29]

Patton disagreed with Eisenhower's desire to rid the Nazis from all power despite the risks of destabilizing Germany's infrastructure. When Eisenhower asked to visit Patton's camps for displaced persons, Patton was surprised, since to him, displaced persons—particularly the Jews whom he said "are lower than animals"—were not even human beings. He blamed them for letting themselves sink to such a low level. He could not comprehend that the Nazi system oppressed people for more than a decade, and he could not understand the Holocaust and its effects.[30]

Eisenhower's visit was a disaster for Patton. German guards, some even in their SS uniforms, were still stationed around the camps. It happened to be Yom Kippur, so Eisenhower and Patton visited the camp synagogue, a poorly ventilated room. Patton almost fainted from the stench of the overheated worshipers and later threw up just thinking about it. Patton could no longer hide his hatred of the Jews. He told Eisenhower that they had "no sense of human decency." Eisenhower snapped back, "Shut up, George."[31]

The situation worsened. Angry that other generals with fewer laurels were receiving plum positions back in the states while he sat at a job that bored him, Patton again put his foot in his mouth. At a press conference on September 22, he was asked about denazification. He explained that no Nazis held power in his region, adding that if the tables were turned and the United States had been occupied, Republicans and Democrats would have been denied their jobs. Firing a country's administrators will only result in turmoil he said. It was more important, he told them, to revive Germany's economy.

The U.S. press seized on this statement, accusing Patton of comparing the Nazis to the Democrats and Republicans. Stories spread, asking whether Patton knew why the war had been fought. Eisenhower was disturbed and called Patton, who assured his commander he had been misquoted. Eisenhower asked him to hold another press conference to set the record straight. Patton agreed and even wrote a speech to deliver. But he strayed from the text and ended up repeating his accusation. He claimed most Germans simply gave the Nazi Party lip service in order to keep their jobs. It was as simple as that, and to deny them work now would retard Bavaria's economic recovery.

Displeased with Patton's second effort, Eisenhower sent for him again. Patton knew he was in trouble and tried to pass off the quotes, as the newspapers had printed them, as the work of Jews and communists angling for his downfall before the next war, which he saw as "on the way." He had clearly become delusional.[32] Eisenhower relieved Patton of command of the Third Army and assigned him command of the Fifteenth Army, which was responsible for compiling and writing the lessons of the war. Patton agreed to the new assignment but hated giving up his beloved Third Army. Lucian Truscott took command on October 7. Patton gave a farewell speech to the gathered soldiers at the change of command ceremony. "All good things must come to an end. The best thing that has ever come to me thus far is the honor and privilege of having commanded the Third Army." When he finished his remarks, Truscott escorted him to the train that would take him to his new job.[33]

Patton enjoyed his time with the Fifteenth Army. His post allowed him to once again concentrate his energies on war, free from politics.

Yet he still complained to his wife and vented to his diary about Eisenhower's leadership and the spread of communism. "I really shudder for the future of our country."[34]

With the Fifteenth Army hard at work, Patton took a nostalgic tour through the countries he had liberated a year before. He received awards in Paris, Rennes, Chartres, and other cities. He was decorated by the Belgian king and attended ceremonies in Metz, Reims, and Luxembourg, where he garnered more awards. He went to Copenhagen and then to Sweden, where he visited the surviving members of the Swedish team in the 1912 Olympic Games. On November 11 he celebrated his birthday with a small crowd and a large pentagon-shaped cake. People told him how good he looked, though he had just turned sixty. He was becoming the Patton of old.

Patton spent most of November writing his "Notes on Combat" and then decided to go home for Christmas to talk to Beatrice about his future. If he was offered a good Army job in the United States, he would stay in the service; if not, he would retire. He would head home on December 10.

The day before his departure, Patton decided to hunt pheasant near Mannheim. He took off in his chauffeured limousine, accompanied by Gen. Hap Gay. A Jeep drove behind them, carrying a hunting dog. On the way, they stopped to view some Roman ruins. Patton muddied his boots and, getting back in the limousine, took them off. The car stopped at a railroad intersection while they waited for a train to pass. Starting up again, they collided with an oncoming Army truck as it took a left turn across their path. The crash threw Patton from his seat. His head grazed the diamond-shaped light on the roof, tearing the skin off the top of his head, and he smashed face first into the driver's partition. He ended up with a broken nose and neck and was paralyzed from the neck down. No one else received as much as a scratch in the accident.[35]

Patton was taken to a hospital in Heidelberg, where doctors stitched up his head and fixed his nose. His neck injury was much more serious. His third and fourth cervical vertebrae were fractured and dislocated. He was placed in traction and doctors hoped for the best. A noted British neurosurgeon was flown in from Oxford University, but there was nothing more for him to do.[36]

When Beatrice found out about her husband's condition, she wanted to go to him. Eisenhower put a plane at her disposal, and she flew to Heidelberg with Dr. R. Glen Spurling, the leading American neurosurgeon. Patton greeted his wife cheerfully yet calmly. He said the only pain he was experiencing was from the two large hooks that had been inserted under his cheekbones and attached to a weight behind his head, keeping him immobilized.

When he had Spurling alone, Patton asked about the truth of his condition. He asked what the chances were that he would be able to ride a horse again. Spurling was direct. "None," he said. "In other words," Patton responded, "the best I could hope for would be semi-invalidism." Again Spurling was direct: "Yes."[37] Patton appreciated the doctor's honesty, but as he thought of his condition, he became depressed, especially at night when only his nurses were present. He managed to stay jovial for guests during the day, but all he wanted to do, he told his nurses, was sleep.

Patton's accident was big news, knocking the Nuremburg trials off the newspapers' front pages. The hospital tried to keep up with the crush of reporters wanting to know his condition. Beatrice handled the hungry reporters and also the mail. He received get-well messages from friends, including Eisenhower and President Harry S Truman.

Immobile and helpless, Patton lingered for thirteen days; his strong constitution keeping him alive. But it was not enough. On December 21 Bea spent most of the day reading to him. At 4:00 p.m. he dozed off and his breathing became irregular. When his respiration improved, Bea and Dr. Spurling went out to dinner. A messenger retrieved them at the restaurant twenty-five minutes later, and when they arrived at the hospital they found Patton dead. The official cause of death was "pulmonary edema and congestive heart failure."[38]

Spurling said that Patton had died the way he lived—bravely. He never complained, followed orders without question, and was kind to everyone in the hospital. "He was a model patient." In Patton's honor, flags were flown at half-mast for the weekend and service clubs for soldiers were closed.[39]

On December 22, the day after his death, Patton's body was placed in state in a nearby villa. Many people filed through to pay their respects to the warrior. The next day the casket was closed and taken to the Heidelberg Protestant Church, escorted by cavalry and pallbearers. After a service, Patton's coffin was placed on a train bound for the American military cemetery in Hamm, Luxembourg. The train stopped six times along the way so that honor guards could place wreaths on the casket. Beatrice reviewed the troops at each stop and offered a few words of sympathy to the crowds.

The next day the cortege made its way though the city streets of Hamm in the rain. Soldiers and civilians watched solemnly. An Army plane, with Gen. Walton Walker on board, circled above as a religious service and military ceremony were conducted. General Walker had been one of Patton's corps commanders and good friend; he had flown in from the states but the weather conditions prevented him from landing. Patton was buried under a white cross marker, similar to the others around him, in the midst of rows of crosses and Stars of David.[40]

So many people visited Patton's burial site over the next three years that the foot traffic killed the grass on his and the surrounding graves. Often after a weekend of visitors the lawn covering the area from the cemetery path to Patton's grave would be depleted by six inches and would require resodding. To resolve the situation, his body was moved to the front of the cemetery. There, just below a low wall overlooking the cemetery and between two U.S. flags, he reposes at the head of his combat dead.

8

His Meaning and Legacy

In 1972 Martin Blumenson opened his first volume of *The Patton Papers* with "everything that anyone has ever said about George S. Patton, Jr., is probably true." Patton was a brilliant battlefield commander, yet he was not infallible. He fit in with high society, yet he could be vulgar. He was passionate about his beliefs, both philosophical and spiritual, yet he had his demons. He praised his fellow officers when they did well, yet cursed them in his diaries and letters. For all his successes there were failures, and for all his brilliance there were mistakes. But in the end, he proved to be a man who knew how to win, how to combine strategy with inspiration, technology with basic human nature.

Throughout his military career Patton was always on the cusp of state-of-the-art thinking. In his early career he experimented with a machine-gun sled and developed the Patton sword. In Mexico he led the first-ever attack from motor-driven vehicles. In World War I, he created, from scratch, the doctrine for American tank tactics as well as a tank school and led his tanks onto the battlefield in their first successful attack. Between wars, in the mock wars of Louisiana and Tennessee, he showed what tanks could do. In World War II, he put mobile warfare theories into practice and showed that an aggressive thrust could defeat the enemy with lighter casualties than could static tactics.

Throughout his early career, Patton benefited from advice and examples from contemporary Army leaders, particularly John J. Pershing, as well most generals from history, whose memoirs he read constantly. By World War II, Patton the student had become Patton the master. He became a leader, innovator, and strategist. He led a green army onto the shores of North Africa and captured Casablanca with minimal casualties. He rejuvenated a defeated II Corps and led it successfully into a war of firepower and maneuver against the Germans. In Sicily he raced across the island while his British counterpart slugged up the east coast. He employed a major airborne operation, armored thrusts, and amphibious assaults to capture Gela, Palermo, and Messina ahead of the British, proving his worth and the value of the American soldier.

In Europe, he exploited a hole in the German lines and turned a minor gain into a double-edged sweeping attack that liberated Brittany as well as most of the rest of France. Had his superiors listened to him and let him proceed, the net cast in Falaise might have bagged even more Germans. Patton continued his American-style blitzkrieg until he was slowed to a crawl as he outran his fuel supplies and encountered harsher terrain, deteriorating weather, and a coordinated enemy defense. He continued to push forward despite these obstacles, and his refusal to go on the defensive kept the Germans in his sector off balance. When the enemy launched its largest counterattack of the war at the Bulge, Patton saw it coming and not only prepared for it but was also the only Army commander to go on the immediate attack. His relief of the surrounded Bastogne was the single greatest defeat to the Germans in the entire Ardennes offensive. With the Bulge closed he raced across a defeated Germany, penetrating both Austria and Czechoslovakia by the time the Germans surrendered.

From 1942 until 1945 Patton repeatedly led the attack. Could anyone else have rejuvenated an entire corps in less than ten days and then lead it successfully on the battlefield? Or outraced an experienced army in Sicily and cover twice as much ground as his rival? What about using the Navy for amphibious end runs? No commander in World War I had attempted it, so a young Patton could not have learned these maneuvers from his predecessors. He simply went off the map when the precedents did not suit him, much as he had in the Louisiana Maneuvers. Could anyone else have exploited the situation in France to change the nature of fighting there? And in December, could any other commander have changed his attack from the east to north in only a few days in the middle of the winter? It is hard to believe one man accomplished so much in one theater of war.

Patton learned that battlefield success was not enough for a twentieth-century warrior. His slapping of two soldiers in Sicily, his willingness to speak about politics, and his ill-advised attempt to rescue his son-in-law from a German POW camp seriously jeopardized his career. While the incidents could have been excused by stress, bad luck, and personal desire, Patton had little regret about all three.

In Sicily, as on any battlefield, some soldiers had shirked their responsibilities and refused to move forward. Battle fatigue was little understood. In addition, Patton was leading a mostly green army whose failures put him on edge. By the time he reached England he was already a celebrity. Everyone wanted a piece of him. It was almost inevitable that he would stray somewhere, even though he always asked that his presence be kept secret. As for the Hammelburg raid, if he had pulled it off, it would have added to the Patton legend. In the Philippines, Douglas MacArthur had pulled off a daring raid to save American POWs from the retreating Japanese. Patton felt that the Germans too were weakening and a light force could accomplish the same goal.

Of the three incidents, the Hammelburg raid was Patton's only battlefield mistake. While he was stalled in Metz prior to the Ardennes offensive, Hammelburg was purely bad judgment. But Patton was human. Other great generals in American history have also failed at times during a successful campaign. George Washington failed at Brandywine, Ulysses S. Grant at Cold Harbor, and Robert E. Lee at Gettysburg. No one who risks great success on the battlefield is immune to failure.

How successful an army commander was Patton? Consider this: by the end of World War II six American armies were stationed in Europe, including Patton's Third. The other five were the First Army, commanded by Courtney Hodges; the Fifth Army, commanded by Lucien Truscott; the Seventh Army, commanded by Alexander "Sandy" Patch; the Ninth Army, commanded by William Simpson; and the Fifteenth Army, commanded by Leonard Gerow. Omar Bradley commanded the First Army for two months and had managed to get it ashore in Normandy and inland before moving up to army group command. Mark Clark had commanded the Fifth Army for fifteen months in Italy before he too was promoted. His Italian campaign can hardly be considered daring and dynamic.

Few if any of those names are recognized as well as Patton's and none were identified as easily with their armies as Patton was with the Third. Courtney Hodges's army held the German counterattack at Mortain while Patton struck across France. Hodges's army also took the blow from the Germans in the Battle of the Bulge while Patton raced to relieve him. And although the First Army fought for two months longer than Patton's Third, it captured fewer prisoners.

Sandy Patch and William Simpson were both fine, capable commanders, but Patch was not in the major field of operations. He was farthest from the vital heart of Germany and did not face the heavier enemy divisions fighting in the north. Simpson was stymied by his group commander, Field Marshal Montgomery.[1] Simpson, whose army was not activated until September 1944, did, however, have the foresight to assign some of his staff members to Patton's headquarters to see how it fought. Truscott became an army commander in Italy in the last month of 1944, and although he led his men well, Italy had by that time proved itself a forgotten theater in Europe. Mark Clark's failures had already identified him with the Fifth Army despite Truscott's successes. Gerow's Fifteenth Army defended rear areas in the war's last four months.

None of these commanders had Patton's flair for the dramatic or his savvy for quotes. None had the amount of experience Patton possessed at the start of the war, and none, save Clark, commanded armies either as long or as successfully.

Statues of Patton stand across the United States, from Boston to Sacramento. Across Europe statues and memorials of Patton and his Third Army stand from France to Czechoslovakia. The famed "victory milestones" that mark every kilometer of liberated territory from Normandy, France, to Bastogne, Belgium, all bear the Third Army symbol.

After his death, Patton continued to influence military thought. Omar Bradley called MacArthur's amphibious attack at Inchon during the Korean War "Pattonesque."[2] In Vietnam, Patton's son, George IV, continued his father's legacy as the commander of the 15th Armored Cavalry. He later went on to command the 2nd Armored Division, giving the unit the nickname "Patton's Own." Norman Schwarzkopf's "Hail Mary" blitz across the Iraqi desert in the first Persian Gulf War was reminiscent of Patton's race across France, though this time it was called the "AirLand Battle" and incorporated technology not available to Patton in the 1940s. Gen. Tommy Franks, before his race to Baghdad in 2003, briefed his staff on Patton's principles of maneuver and speed in his race across France and in the Battle of the Bulge.[3] Today, Carlo D'Este's *Patton: A Genius for War* is required reading at the Army's Officer Candidate School, while Patton's tactics are still taught at the armor school at Fort Knox.

Scores of books have been written about Patton for both the armor student, history scholar, and the casual reader, but possibly nothing has done more to sear Patton into the public's mind than the 1970 movie *Patton* starring George C. Scott. The image of Scott standing in front of an American flag while delivering one of Patton's rousing speeches is more imbedded in the American psyche than any photo of the general himself. The image has been used and parodied endlessly to the point that it is now cliché.

Who was George S. Patton? He was an individual of enormous drive and energy who loved the vocation of war. To him war was not a grim and necessary business but an adventure that brought out the best in people and was filled with heroics and bravery. Every brush with death made him feel more alive. Time spent at the rear in a headquarters only made him chafe for the front. While other generals read paperback novels to escape the pressures of combat, he read military histories, gleaning lessons of leadership and strategy. He also knew how to push his men. They may have loved him or hated him, but they fought for him. And strangely enough, when the world no longer needed his services, he exited the stage.

Since his childhood George S. Patton had wanted to be soldier on a battlefield. He succeeded in World War I by leading the most cutting-edge technology into the field against the enemy. He surpassed his own ambitions by becoming the most successful army commander in the Allied cause in the last great war of the twentieth century. His tactics, passion, and dedication to his vocation helped win the war in Europe faster and with fewer Allied casualties. He will always be remembered as one of America's greatest military commanders.

Notes

Preface
1. Martin Blumenson, *The Patton Papers* (Boston: Houghton Mifflin, 1975), 2: 46.
2. Ruth Ellen Patton Totten, *The Button Box: A Daughter's Loving Memoir of Mrs. George S. Patton*, ed. John Patton Totten (Columbia: University of Missouri Press, 2005), 94–95.
3. Ladislas Farago, *Patton: Ordeal and Triumph* (New York: I. Obolensky, 1964), 31 and 241.
4. Robert N. Patton, *The Pattons: A Personal History of an American Family* (New York: Crown Publishers, 1994), 268–69.
5. Blumenson, *Patton Papers*, 2: 662.
6. Ibid., 2: 832.
7. Carlo D'Este, *Patton: A Genius for War* (New York: Harper Collins, 1995), 8.
8. Stanley P. Hirshon, *General Patton: A Soldier's Life* (New York: Harper Collins, 2005), 6.

Chapter 1
1. D'Este, *Patton*, 18.
2. Blumenson, *The Patton Papers*, 1: 27.
3. Patton, *The Pattons*, 37–59.
4. Blumenson, *Patton Papers*, 1: 24.
5. D'Este, *Patton*, 28.
6. Patton, *The Pattons*, 98.
7. Hirshon, *General Patton*, 17.

8. Patton, *The Pattons*, 82.
9. Blumenson, *Patton Papers*, 1: 32.
10. D'Este, *Patton*, 40.
11. Patton, *The Pattons*, 72.
12. D'Este, *Patton*, 40–42.
13. Ibid., 44.
14. Patton, *The Pattons*, 90–93.
15. Ibid., 94–95.
16. Ibid., 99.
17. Blumenson, *Patton Papers*, 1: 38–40.
18. Ibid., 40–41.
19. Patton, *The Pattons*, 114–15.
20. Totten, *Button Box*, 66–68.
21. Ibid., 30–31; Patton, *The Pattons*, 102.
22. Blumenson, *Patton Papers*, 1: 49.
23. Ibid., 51–52.
24. Ibid., 58.

Chapter 2
1. Blumenson, *Patton Papers*, 1: 61.
2. Patton, *The Pattons*, 116, 7.[**Au: Do you mean 116–17?**]
3. Blumenson, *Patton Papers*, 1: 61–62.
4. Totten, *Button Box*, 70.
5. Patton, *The Pattons*, 120.
6. Blumenson, *Patton Papers*, 1: 84–85.
7. Ibid., 86.
8. Ibid., 88.
9. Ibid., 89.
10. Ibid., 90.
11. Ibid., 94, 128–29.
12. Totten, *Button Box*, 71.
13. Blumenson, *Patton Papers*, 1: 98, 103–104.
14. Ibid., 113.
15. Ibid., 118.
16. Patton, *The Pattons*, 123.
17. D'Este, *Patton,* 86.

18. Blumenson, *Patton Papers*, 1: 119, 124, 125.
19. D'Este, *Patton,* 89–90.
20. Ibid., 90–91.
21. Totten, *Button Box*, 73.
22. Ibid., 78.
23. Blumenson, *Patton Papers*, 1: 157–58.

Chapter 3
1. Patton, *The Pattons*, 137–39.
2. Ibid., 139; and Blumenson, *Patton Papers*, 1: 200–201.
3. Totten, *Button Box*, 78–79.
4. D'Este, *Patton*, 112.
5. Martin Blumenson, *Patton: The Man Behind the Legend, 1885–1945* (New York: Morrow, 1985), 63.
6. Totten, *Button Box*, 85–86.
7. Blumenson, *Patton*, 68–69.
8. D'Este, *Patton*, 121–22.
9. Blumenson, *Patton*, 70.
10. Totten, *Button Box*, 89–90.
11. Patton, *The Pattons*, 142; and Blumenson, *Patton Papers*, 1: 212.
12. D'Este, *Patton*, 130.
13. Totten, *Button Box*, 96.
14. Patton, *The Pattons*, 142.
15. D'Este, *Patton*, 162.
16. Herbert Molloy Jr., *The Great Pursuit: Pershing's Expedition to Destroy Pancho Villa* (New York: Konecky & Konecky, 1970), 84.
17. Patton, *The Pattons*, 153–55.
18. Ibid., 108.
19. D'Este, *Patton*, 163.
20. Blumenson, *Patton Papers*, 1: 400.
21. Ibid., 401–405.
22. D'Este, *Patton,* 197.
23. Blumenson, *Patton Papers*, 1: 464.
24. Ibid., 463.
25. Blumenson, *Patton,* 103.
26. Blumenson, *Patton Papers*, 1: 508–509.

27. Blumenson, *Patton*, 106.

28. Blumenson, *Patton Papers*, 1: 540–41.

29. Ibid., 587–89.

30. Kevin Hymel, *Patton's Photographs: War as He Saw It* (Washington, DC: Potomac Books, 2006), 65–67.

31. Blumenson, *Patton Papers*, 1: 609.

32. Ibid., 612.

33. Ibid., 613.

34. Ibid., 636–37.

Chapter 4

1. D'Este, *Patton*, 287.

2. John Eisenhower, *General Ike: A Personal Reminiscence* (New York: Free Press, 2003), 1, 2.

3. D'Este, *Patton*, 293.

4. Blumenson, *Patton*, 123, 124.

5. D'Este, *Patton*, 331.

6. Blumenson, *Patton*, 125.

7. Patton, *The Pattons*, 210–11.

8. Blumenson, *Patton*, 128.

9. Ibid., 130.

10. D'Este, *Patton*, 349–50.

11. Patton, *The Pattons*, 212–13.

12. Blumenson, *Patton Papers*, 1: 893–97; and Patton, *The Pattons*, 213.

13. Totten, *Button Box*, 245–47.

14. Blumenson, *Patton*, 136.

15. Hirshon, *General Patton*, 214.

16. Patton, *The Pattons*, 234–35.

17. Totten, *Button Box*, 286.

18. Ibid., 290.

19. Blumenson, *Patton Papers*, 1: 931–34.

20. Blumenson, *Patton*, 141.

21. D'Este, *Patton*, 380.

22. Blumenson, *Patton Papers*, 2: 16–17.

23. Farago, *Patton*, 162–64.

24. D'Este, *Patton*, 406.

25. Blumenson, *Patton*, 161.

26. Ibid., 163.

27. Blumenson, *Patton Papers*, 2: 79.

28. Hirshon, *General Patton*, 264–65.

29. Blumenson, *Patton*, 165.

30. Blumenson, *Patton Papers*, 2: 80–81.

31. Blumenson, *Patton*, 165.

32. Blumenson, *Patton Papers*, 2: 87.

33. Blumenson, *Patton*, 168.

Chapter 5

1. Blumenson, *Patton*, 169.

2. D'Este, *Patton*, 435

3. Hymel, *Patton's Photographs*, 11–12.

4. D'Este, *Patton*, 437–38.

5. Blumenson, *Patton Papers*, 2: 110.

6. Farago, *Patton*, 214–16.

7. Hymel, *Patton's Photographs*, 8.

8. Blumenson, *Patton*, 174.

9. Hirshon, *General Patton*, 288.

10. Hymel, *Patton's Photographs*, 16.

11. Ibid., 20.

12. Blumenson, *Patton*, 176.

13. Blumenson, *Patton Papers*, 2: 138–39.

14. D'Este, *Patton*, 456–57.

15. Blumenson, *Patton*, 177.

16. D'Este, *Patton*, 452.

17. Blumenson, *Patton*, 181.

18. Blumenson, *Patton Papers*, 2: 177.

19. Ibid., 178.

20. Farago, *Patton*, 242–43.

21. Blumenson, *Patton*, 182–83.

22. Hymel, *Patton's Photographs*, 22.

23. Blumenson, *Patton Papers*, 2: 188.

24. Ibid., 198.

25. D'Este, *Patton*, 477.
26. Blumenson, *Patton*, 188.
27. D'Este, *Patton*, 479–81.
28. Blumenson, *Patton Papers*, 2: 211–12.
29. Ibid., 197; and Hymel, *Patton's Photographs*, 25–26.
30. Blumenson, *Patton*, 189.
31. Farago, *Patton*, 272.
32. D'Este, *Patton*, 495–506.
33. Blumenson, *Patton Papers*, 2: 274–75.
34. Blumenson, *Patton*, 195.
35. Farago, *Patton*, 299–230.
36. Hymel, *Patton's Photographs*, 32–33.
37. Ibid., 33–34.
38. Blumenson, *Patton Papers*, 2: 284.
39. Ibid., 285.
40. Blumenson, *Patton*, 199.
41. Hymel, *Patton's Photographs*, 29, 36–37.
42. Ibid., 35.
43. Ibid., 37.
44. Blumenson, *Patton Papers*, 2: 301–302.
45. Douglas Porch, *The Path to Victory: The Mediterranean Theater in World War II* (New York: Farrar, Straus, and Giroux, 2004), 442.
46. Farago, *Patton*, 334–35.
47. Blumenson, *Patton Papers*, 2: 203.[Au: correct vol. and page number?]
48. Ibid., 2: 323.
49. Ibid., 333–34.
50. Omar Bradley and Clay Blair, *A General's Life: An Autobiography* (New York: Simon & Shuster, 1983), 198.
51. David Eisenhower, *Eisenhower at War, 1943–1945* (New York: Random House, 1986), 37–38.
52. Hymel, *Patton's Photographs*, 46–49.
53. Blumenson, *Patton*, 214–15.
54. Blumenson, *Patton Papers*, 2: 388.
55. D'Este, *Patton*, 560.
56. Hymel, *Patton's Photographs*, 50.
57. Blumenson, *Patton*, 216.

58. Ibid., 220.
59. Blumenson, *Patton Papers*, 2: 427.
60. Hymel, *Patton's Photographs*, 45.
61. Blumenson, *Patton*, 221–22.

Chapter 6
 1. Blumenson, *Patton Papers*, 2: 480.
 2. Hymel, *Patton's Photographs*, 59–61.
 3. Bradley and Blair, *General's Life*, 279–81.
 4. Hymel, *Patton's Photographs*, 61–62.
 5. Blumenson, *Patton*, 229.
 6. D'Este, *Patton*, 628.
 7. Blumenson, *Patton Papers*, 2: 497–98.
 8. Martin Blumeson, *The Duel for France, 1944: The Men and Battles That Changed the Fate of Europe* (Cambridge, MA: Da Capo, 2000), 228.
 9. Blumenson, *Duel for France*, 258–59.
10. Blumenson, *Patton Papers*, 2: 510.
11. Blumenson, *Duel for France*, 276–88.
12. Blumenson, *Patton*, 236.
13. Blumenson, *Patton Papers*, 2: 522.
14. D'Este, *Patton*, 647.
15. Blumenson, *Patton*, 238.
16. Blumenson, *Patton Papers*, 2: 203; and D'Este, *Patton*, 662.
17. Hymel, *Patton's Photographs*, 67–68.
18. Ibid., 71; and Blumenson, *Patton Papers*, 2: 558.
19. Blumenson, *Patton Papers*, 2: 567.
20. Blumenson, *Patton*, 244.
21. Hymel, *Patton's Photographs*, 72.
22. Blumenson, *Patton Papers*, 2: 572–73.
23. D. A. Lande, *I Was With Patton: First-Person Accounts of WWII in George S. Patton's Command* (St. Paul: MBI Publishing, 2002), 169–70.
24. Blumenson, *Patton Papers*, 2: 577–78.
25. Ibid., 576.
26. Ibid., 585–86.

27. Ibid., 582.
28. Charles Codman, *Drive* (Boston: Little, Brown, 1957), 230.
29. Bradley and Blair, *General's Life*, 358.
30. Codman, *Drive*, 232.
31. D'Este, *Patton*, 684.
32. Hymel, *Patton's Photographs*, 83.
33. Blumenson, *Patton Papers*, 2: 606.
34. Hymel, *Patton's Photographs*, 77, 82.
35. Blumenson, *Patton Papers*, 2: 609; and Lande, *I Was With Patton*, 203–204.
36. Blumenson, *Patton Papers*, 2: 614–16.
37. Blumenson, *Patton Papers*, 2: 620.
38. Lande, *I Was With Patton*, 213–14.
39. Hymel, *Patton's Photographs*, 78.
40. Blumenson, *Patton Papers*, 2: 627.

Chapter 7
1. Blumenson, *Patton Papers*, 2: 633.
2. Hymel, *Patton's Photographs*, 91, 93.
3. Lande, *I Was With Patton*, 224.
4. Blumenson, *Patton*, 253–56.
5. D'Este, *Patton*, 710–11.
6. Blumenson, *Patton Papers*, 2: 656–57.
7. Ibid., 654.
8. Hymel, *Patton's Photographs*, 96–97.
9. Blumenson, *Patton Papers*, 2: 660; and Hymel, *Patton's Photographs*, 98.
10. D'Este, *Patton*, 712.
11. Blumenson, *Patton*, 260–61.
12. Hymel, *Patton's Photographs*, 101–102.
13. Blumenson, *Patton Papers*, 2: 673–75.
14. Blumenson, *Patton*, 264.
15. Blumenson, *Patton Papers*, 2: 683.
16. Lande, *I Was With Patton*, 239.
17. Blumenson, *Patton Papers*, 2: 690.
18. Hymel, *Patton's Photographs*, 93.

19. Ibid., 100–105.
20. Blumenson, *Patton Papers*, 2: 697.
21. Hymel, *Patton's Photographs*, 111–13.
22. D'Este, *Patton*, 740.
23. Blumenson, *Patton*, 270.
24. Blumenson, *Patton Papers*, 2: 716.
25. D'Este, *Patton*, 746–47.
26. Ibid., 749.
27. Blumenson, *Patton Papers*, 2: 735.
28. Blumenson, *Patton*, 280.
29. Ibid., 281.
30. D'Este, *Patton*, 755.
31. Ladislas Farago, *The Last Days of Patton* (New York: Berkley Books, 1981), 159–60.
32. Blumenson, *Patton*, 288.
33. Blumenson, *Patton Papers*, 2: 792–93.
34. Blumenson, *Patton*, 289.
35. Farago, *Last Days*, 224–29; and D'Este, *Patton*, 786.
36. Farago, *Last Days*, 236.
37. Blumenson, *Patton Papers*, 2: 825.
38. Farago, *Last Days*, 272.
39. Blumenson, *Patton*, 296.
40. Blumenson, *Patton Papers*, 2: 835.

Chapter 8

1. Clay Blair, *Ridgway's Paratroopers: The American Airborne in World War II.* (New York: The Dial Press, 1995), 470–471.
2. Bradley and Blair, *General's Life*, 556.
3. Tommy Franks, *American Soldier*, with Malcolm McConnell (New York: Regan Books, 2004), 400.

Both authors have written biographies of Gen. George S. Patton. Martin Blumenson's *The Patton Papers*, vols. 1 and 2 (Boston: Houghton Mifflin, 1972–75), are considered the bible for any study of the general. The papers are comprised of Patton's letters and diary entries as well as interviews, press conference transcripts, and enemy documents. Blumenson added context to the materials by setting the historic scene or providing background on the players of Patton's story. Blumenson also wrote *Patton: The Man Behind the Legend, 1885–1945* (New York: Morrow, 1985), which examines Patton's development as a soldier and his relations with other officers, from General Pershing to Eisenhower and Bradley.

Kevin Hymel wrote *Patton's Photographs: War as He Saw It* (Washington, D.C.: Potomac Books, 2006), a picture book of the photographs Patton took during World War II. Hymel composed the book from Patton's photo albums, which included captions and letters that could not be found in any other Patton materials.

The best primary source of information about Patton can be found at the Library of Congress in Washington, D.C. The library's Manuscripts Division holds Patton's letters and diaries as well as his photo albums. Patton's autobiography of his experiences in World War II, *War as I Knew It*, annotated by Paul D. Harkins (Boston: Houghton Mifflin, 1947), came primarily from the materials in the Library of Congress. Patton also worked on it during the war's closing days, and his wife, Beatrice, completed the work for publication.

Other books help illuminate Patton and his soldierly career as well as his family. Possibly the best single volume biography on Patton comes from Carlo D'Este. His *Patton: A Genius for War* (New York: Harper

Collins, 1995) is meticulously researched and gives a thorough exami-
nation of Patton and his role in American history. *Patton: Ordeal and
Triumph* by Ladislas Farago (New York: I. Obolensky, 1964), on which
the movie *Patton* was based, was one of the first serious overviews of
Patton's life and translates well today. *General Patton: A Soldier's Life* by
Stanley Hirshon (New York: Harper Collins, 2005) belittles the general
and his accomplishments, yet provides new primary materials to tell
Patton's story. *Patton and Rommel: Men of War in the Twentieth Century*
by Dennis Showalter (New York: Berkley Caliber, 2005) provides a dual
biography of both Patton and the German commander he wished most
to face in battle, Field Marshal Irwin Rommel.

Three books delve into Patton's role in World War II. *The Armies of
George S. Patton* by George Forty (London: Arms and Armour, 1996)
breaks down the units that served under Patton from the battles in North
Africa until the end of the war. It also explains the staff positions of
Patton's armies and provides biographies of his commanders and his
staff. *Patton at Bay: The Lorraine Campaign, September to December,
1944* by John Nelson Rickard (Westport, CT: Praeger, 1999) examines
Patton and his Third Army during the slugging match along the Ger-
man border in 1944. *I Was With Patton* by Dave Lande (St. Paul: MBI
Publishing, 2002) looks at Patton through the eyes of the men who
fought under him from the Louisiana Maneuvers to the end of World
War II.

To understand Patton, the man, and his family, there are three excellent books. *The Fighting Pattons* by Brian Sobel (Westport, CT: Praeger,
1997) looks at Patton and his son, Maj. Gen. George S. Patton (ret.),
and the similarities and differences of their experiences at war and peace.
The Pattons: A Personal History of an American Family by Robert Patton
(New York: Crown Publishers, 1994) examines the history of the Patton
family from its arrival in North America to the generation of Patton's
grandchildren, who grew up with the responsibilities and under the
pressure of being Pattons. *The Button Box: A Daughter's Loving Memoir
of Mrs. George S. Patton* by Ruth Ellen Patton Totten and edited by her
son James Patton Totten (Columbia: University of Missouri Press, 2005)
provides an interesting perspective of Patton, through the eyes of his
wife, Beatrice.

Index

About the Authors

Martin Blumenson was born in New York City, New York, and raised in Bernardsville, New Jersey. He earned degrees at Bucknell and Harvard universities. He served in the U.S. Army in Europe with the Third Army Headquarters during World War II, in command of the 3rd Historical Detachment in Korea, as chief historian of Joint Task Seven for the atomic weapons tests in the Pacific in 1956, and with the Chief of Military History in Washington, D.C. He was a visiting professor at the Army, Naval, and National War colleges; the Citadel; and Acadia, Bucknell, and George Washington universities, as well as the University of Texas–Austin and the University of North Texas. The author of eighteen books, he lived in Washington, D.C., until his death in 2005.

Kevin M. Hymel is the research director for *World War II History* and *Military Heritage* magazines. He has written numerous articles for each. He is also the author of *Patton's Photographs: War as He Saw It* (Washington, D.C.: Potomac Books, 2006). He is a battlefield tour guide for Stephen Ambrose Historical Tours and leads a tour on General Patton's European battlefields. He received degrees from LaSalle and Villanova universities and lives in Arlington, Virginia.